KV-510-166

Contents

The Art of Surviving in Supply Teaching

Martin Dougherty

David Fulton Publishers
London

David Fulton Publishers Ltd
Ormond House, 26–27 Boswell Street, London WC1N 3JD

First published in Great Britain by David Fulton Publishers 1998

British Library Cataloguing in Publication Data
A catalogue record for this book is available from the British Library

ISBN 1-85346-508-9

Typeset by Textype Typesetters, Cambridge
Printed in Great Britain by The Cromwell Press, Trowbridge

Preface

Upon completing my teaching Degree, I knew a fair amount about many aspects of teaching – or at least the theory involved. How much I did not know would soon be made apparent by the classes I taught in my first years. But I was at least adequately prepared to confront most of the challenges that meet a new physics teacher: Educational Psychology; Special Needs; Classroom Management; Specialist Knowledge – all of these, and others, I had at least some knowledge of.

Yet there was an area which had not been addressed during my training. I knew next to nothing about Supply teaching, and everything that I knew turned out to be wrong. For whatever it worth; all I knew was that 'Supply Teachers earn £88 per day.' This 'fact' turned out to be incorrect, and was the sum total of knowledge imparted to me by lecturing staff. This lack of guidance becomes all the more alarming when one considers that nowadays many Supply teachers are young, often newly-qualified.

Perhaps the assumption is made that student teachers do not immediately become Supply teachers. By the time an NQT becomes a Supply teacher, He or she will have many years' experience in mainstream classroom teaching. This assumption turned out to be quite wrong in my case. My first job was as a Supply teacher working through an agency, a story repeated by many newly-qualified teachers gaining experience or while looking around for a permanent post.

The accompanying, unspoken, assumption, that any good teacher can 'figure out' how to be a good Supply teacher, has in my experience generally turned out to be true – with a few unfortunate exceptions. But is Supply really so similar to mainstream teaching that one can leap the gap without making any mistakes along the way? How long does it take to make the adjustment? How much damage can one do to one's own employment prospects and the education of the nation's youth in the meantime? However good a teacher one may be, there are differences between working in Supply and mainstream teaching. The 'business' side also needs to be considered, and a mainstream teacher has no experience to guide him or her. I cannot deny that a good teacher can make the adjustment in time. My intent is to make that time as short as possible.

In this book I hope to present the products of my own 'learning curve', the distilled essence of several years' experience – mistakes and all – in the classroom and the marketplace. Much of what you will find in here is applicable to a Teaching Practice or a new post, as well as to Supply teaching.

There is no impressive theory in here, nor quotations from the great educational thinkers, though much of the content of this books echoed in the DfE circular 7/97 Use of Supply Teaching. Instead what I have written is intended to be immediately accessible and useable to the pushed-for-time teacher. By providing workable rules-of-thumb I hope to help the reader avoid the more obvious pitfalls while learning to capitalise on his or her own strengths, to find more work and to do a better job in the classroom. From finding work to choosing between assignments; from performing in the classroom to staying on in an assignment, surviving in Supply teaching is an art. It must be learned, sometimes the hard way. It cannot really be taught. That said, I know that I could have done with some help while I was learning the art.

I hope, then, to redress the balance a little. There IS some guidance available to Supply teachers, prospective, new or experienced.

Here it is.

CHAPTER ONE

The Need for Temporary Staff

Thinking back to our school days, most of us will be able to remember the sudden appearance of a replacement teacher. This may not have made much of an impression at the time, but most of us have been taught by temporary staff at one time or another.

Many pupils have been taught by replacement staff without ever realising that this was the case. Others have memories of supply teachers who were nothing more than qualified persons sitting with a class. While the pupils may receive adequate supervision, little is contributed to their education. Fortunately, many supply staff try hard to do more than just 'be there'. These locums are not permanent members of staff, but they should be dedicated professionals, having in mind some or all of the following considerations:

- the need to extend first-hand experience in schools;
- the sense of self-esteem at giving good value for money;
- the need for appropriately paid employment;
- the duty to serve the interests of the pupils;
- the enhancement of career and future employment prospects.

Good supply teachers do more than just cover a class for a few days. In his or her stay, brief or otherwise, every supply teacher makes an impact on the lives of all the pupils he or she meets. Not only does the quality of the supply teacher's performance affect each child's education, but he or she also affects the perceptions of each pupil, influencing the child's feelings about the teaching profession, the school, the subject taught, and about education in general. Even a short period of cover can leave a lasting impression with the pupils, and can have a profound effect upon their lives – for good or ill.

Supply teaching, then, is more than just a matter of pasting over the cracks and making sure a qualified person is present to look after a class. It is a continuation of the education process and an opportunity to do a great deal of good. The quality of the supply teacher found to cover a particular vacancy is of high importance, though unfortunately there is not always time to match the locum to the precise set of needs that may arise.

The reasons for needing a temporary teacher are many and varied. Within the mainstream of education, the reason is usually the absence, planned or otherwise, of a particular colleague. Most secondary schools will cover absence internally for a few days – usually two or three, although there are other possible arrangements; in primary schools this option may not exist as there are no free staff to handle cover lessons. In this case external cover must be sought immediately. Other reasons for using non-permanent staff include:

- a slight staffing shortfall not great enough to warrant an extra member of staff on a full contract;
- inability to find a teacher willing or able to teach some specialist subject on a permanent basis;
- particular teachers being off timetable for conferences or other reasons;
- circumstances such as the preparation period before inspection.

The usual methods of filling the timetable gap are either to use supply staff on a day-to-day basis or to offer a temporary or part-time contract. The latter is possible where a vacancy exists within the school's timetabling arrangements which can be filled by appointing a member of staff with the usual contract terms, but stipulating a fixed period and probably a reduced teaching commitment. This short-term contract brings the temporary teacher into the school as an employee, just the same as any other member of the school's staff. The contract period can be extended, but the teacher cannot be regarded as casual and be dismissed if the vacancy proves to be of shorter duration than planned.

In many cases this approach is not practicable. It is not legal to offer a contract of employment for a teacher to do someone else's job, even if they are long-term absent with little prospect of ever returning to work. The absent colleague is still employed by the school; it is their post and cannot be given to someone else except on a temporary cover basis. The answer is, of course, to engage a supply teacher.

Most deputy heads, seeking temporary cover, will turn first to their school's supply team, which is generally composed of retirees or those who have left permanent posts to raise a family. Many such are ex-members of the school's own staff, and thus are familiar with the school and many of the pupils. These individuals should be able to fit in well at short notice without needing lengthy induction. Many such teachers have other commitments (educational and personal), or have pension abatement to think about. As a result they may be able to come in for a few days at short notice, but may not be able to take on longer-term work.

In the case of a longer-term absence, it can prove a little more difficult to find a suitable locum. Most retirees do not want to return to full-time work for several months at a stretch. So the deputy head must look elsewhere, to unknown teachers offering their services to schools they have never seen. How can the school judge the suitability of a completely unknown teacher?

It is often possible to obtain recommendations from current staff. Many teachers know someone who they can vouch for, who works on supply. This personal recommendation is not a complete guarantee of quality, but it is certainly a great deal better than bringing in a complete unknown.

Sometimes, for example in the case of maternity leave, there is enough time to advertise in the press. Such advertisements invite applications from interested teachers, and selection can be carried out in a similar manner to recruiting a full-time permanent teacher. Careful selection is important when a teacher is going to be in a temporary post for some months.

This approach is not always possible, however. A common example occurs when a teacher is absent for what is expected to be a short period with no notice, as often happens in the case of sudden illness. While it is possible to muddle through for a few days – and many schools try to do this until the situation becomes a little clearer – if this short absence keeps getting longer it becomes imperative that a good replacement be found for the duration. If there has been no time to advertise and personal recommendation has failed to come up with anyone suitable, what then?

Some LEA pools will try to find a suitable teacher from their lists at the deputy head's request. Many, however, keep nothing more than a list of teachers and require that deputies somehow make contact themselves: generally this means sifting through a pile of old speculative letters from supply teachers seeking work, then telephoning the ones that seem to be the most suitable to find out if they are available. This system is not always satisfactory.

Many deputy heads are now turning to professional agencies in order to find a suitable locum to fill their vacancy. There are advantages and disadvantages to using agencies. The most commonly voiced objections to using agencies are:

- the school will have to pay for the agency's services.
- concern about teachers' terms and conditions of employment being eroded;
- concern that the agency may be putting unsuitable staff out for the sake of profit;

The first point also applies to those LEAs which charge a flat rate no matter what the teacher is actually paid, and is perhaps 'fair enough' considering the benefits of using an agency. The second point is the subject of discussion and agreements between agencies and professional bodies, and the third is almost unheard-of. No reputable agency acts in this manner, nor would any that intended to stay in business. However, some schools and some LEAs have an outright policy of never using agencies. There are plenty of schools for which the opposite is true – and many of these schools set out with 'no agency' policies, being later forced or persuaded to change this attitude due to circumstances, unavailability of suitable cover anywhere else, or recommendation from other deputy heads. The advantages of using an agency are clear enough:

- a single call to the agency office transfers the problem of finding someone to the coordinator there;
- they have large numbers of teachers on their books;
- teachers will have at the very least been interviewed and vetted when they registered with the agency. More likely, they will have worked through the agency in the past and thus have a proven record. The fact that an agency recommends a teacher is, theoretically at least, a guarantee of competence. The DfE Circular 'Use of Supply Teachers' (7/97) states that: 'Schools using agencies should . . . have a written agreement with the agencies specifying the service the agency will provide', and advises on what the agreement should include.

Agency supply teachers are not all retirees or those returning to work after a break. Many are young; some are newly qualified teachers (NQTs) gaining experience. Others are returning to teaching or seeking a reduced commitment while remaining within the profession. Personal circumstances vary, but among all these potential locums it is usually possible to find someone to fit any vacancy. And doing that on demand is what keeps the agency in business.

There are other reasons for employing temporary or casual teaching staff. For example, it is becoming quite common for parents to appoint a tutor for their children, whether for a few weeks or a whole two-year examination course. Private tuition is very different from classroom teaching but it is a useful function for trained teaching staff. Supply staff are sometimes also employed to perform special teaching duties, for example working with problem pupils permanently excluded from school, or with those who cannot attend a mainstream school for whatever reason. Appropriately qualified teaching staff are sometimes employed by those local authorities which run a Special Needs unit outside the mainstream schools. Those teachers who are without a permanent post, for whatever reason, can thus still fulfil a useful function in education.

Indeed, without them the education system would function less efficiently.

The following examples illustrate some of the many arrangements which can be made when supply cover is required:

Case 1:

A secondary school required a teacher to cover two half-days per week in one department. This slight shortfall had previously been covered by a supply teacher who had left upon finding a permanent post elsewhere. Although engaged for only two half-days, the first supply teacher assigned found himself covering an illness for the remainder of the first week in a different department. During the second week, the supply teacher was redeployed to cover a long-term absence in his own subject area. The shortfall was then covered by a succession of supply teachers until one who was suitable was found. He, too, ended up at the school on an almost full-time basis, covering the timetable shortfall and also any other incidental needs which came up – an average of 3-4 full days per week, since such a large school almost always needed cover somewhere. This locum had to be willing to come to work not knowing if he was staying all day or not, nor if he would be required later in the week.

Case 2:

A school had appointed a supply teacher to teach English for the duration of a particular colleague's illness, starting on the first day of the new term. The supply teacher did not turn up, and was eventually telephoned by the somewhat desperate deputy head. Pleading domestic problems, the supply teacher declined to take up his agreed duties. The situation was rather vague, with the absent colleague holding a sick note valid for three more days but not hopeful of returning after this time. By mid-morning, another supply teacher had been recommended, who agreed to cover those three days initially, even though she knew little about teaching English. One sick note followed another, with the supply teacher working full-time for no less than six months in the English department and learning a great deal about English teaching along the way.

Case 3:

With two senior staff long-term absent, it was necessary to reduce the surviving senior staff's contact time so that the others' duties could be covered. The lessons needing cover were scattered about the week, and the chosen supply teacher needed to travel a long distance to reach the school, meaning that half-days were not really feasible. The result was some internal reshuffling, so that a timetable of two full days could be constructed for the supply teacher by moving other teachers' free periods. The timetable so constructed included mainstream classroom teaching as well as special needs support work – a new experience for the locum! This assignment required a certain amount of flexibility on the part of both the locum and the very hard-pressed school in order to strike a balance between cost-effectiveness and staff morale.

CHAPTER TWO
Getting Started

Requirements and qualifications

In order to be employed as a teacher, one must have and be able to prove Qualified Teacher Status. This is awarded upon completion of a recognised teacher training course, normally either a Post-Graduate Certificate of Education (PGCE) or Bachelor of Education (B.Ed) degree. This status is conferred in writing by the Department for Education and Employment (DfEE). The letter itself is proof of a person's competence to teach; without it, it is impossible to gain employment in a mainstream school.

As well as proof of Qualified Teacher Status, a police check is required by law in any profession where one has access to children. This is an attempt to ascertain whether or not an individual is a 'person of good character'. While it is not possible to be completely certain that a prospective teacher is safe to be trusted in charge of children, this check at least gives an assurance that the prospective locum is not, for example, a convicted paedophile.

The police check requires that List 99 be consulted. This list is simply a directory of disqualified teachers who are not to be allowed access to children. Reasons for being placed on List 99 include school-related financial infractions as well as the more obvious breaches of trust such as child abuse or violence.

The second part of the police check requires an investigation into the background of the prospective teacher and any convictions he/she may have. Some minor offences, such as road traffic convictions, have no bearing, but most criminal offences can bar a person from employment as a teacher. For such a sensitive area of employment, convictions are never considered 'spent'. In other words, any previous convictions, and any convictions pending, must be declared at application, however old or irrelevant they may now seem. If a police check unearths undeclared convictions then the teacher is at the very least in breach of contract. Withholding such information can be viewed as suspicious and could lead to prosecution, and will almost certainly result in the teacher being immediately dismissed.

In the event that the police check comes up with convictions that might make the teacher unfit to teach, he/she will be immediately suspended if already teaching. If it later transpires that a mistake has been made, or if it is deemed that the teacher is still fit despite the conviction, a quorum of governors is required to reinstate the teacher.

The police check takes a few weeks to complete. However, it is possible to speed up the process. If one is on record as having passed a police check fairly recently, (say within the previous three years), it might be worth requesting a copy of this data. One is entitled under the Data Protection Act to a copy of any data held. There is a fee for this, but if time is an important factor then this approach is worth considering.

It is possible to have passed these two hurdles, and completed a satisfactory medical check – which any person in reasonable health will pass – and yet be wholly unfit to hold a temporary teaching appointment. Most persons who have completed their training and are in good health with no convictions will be deemed suitable to be considered for a post. However, there is a gulf between being suitable for consideration and being an effective temporary teacher.

Experience is a vital requirement in a temporary teacher. This might seem to rule out NQTs, and indeed many LEA supply pools will not register teachers with less than one year's experience. This is not universally the case, though, and in truth *all* qualified teachers have at least some experience. Even an NQT has the experience gained during short and longer assignments of teaching practice during training. Most teaching staff offering themselves as locums have far more experience, of course, but that is not to say that the NQT cannot be an effective supply teacher. In many ways, supply teaching has more in common with teaching practice than with normal classroom teaching. The permanent, full-time teacher:

- knows that he/she is permanently employed and can plan long-term;
- has a classroom of his/her own and can modify it as desired;
- can arrange resource availability well ahead of time and can order needed items;
- has some influence over curriculum content;
- is generally familiar with classes and pupils, school procedures and staff;

By contrast the locum teacher:

- is not permanent and thus must plan in the short term;
- cannot make lasting changes to the classroom environment;
- inherits someone else's timetable and classes, and must at least initially follow someone else's scheme of work;
- may not be familiar with procedures and staff.

It can thus be seen that the supply teacher has a lot in common with a student teacher beginning a new teaching practice. Many of the same uncertainties apply, and where the NQT has recent memories of having to start a new job, a more experienced teacher – perhaps having held the same post for years – may actually be less flexible.

Obviously, the best sort of experience for supply teaching is experience of temporary teaching gained elsewhere. But one cannot gain this experience without working as a supply teacher. Experience of mainstream classroom teaching is almost as good. The differences between the two styles are marked enough that it is possible to be an excellent classroom teacher yet a very poor supply – but only if the teacher has given up on new ideas and contexts, simply applying what he/she already knows to a situation where it may not be completely effective. Temporary teaching is a different challenge to mainstream classroom teaching, but not so different that it cannot effectively be approached by any experienced teacher. Good practice is always good practice.

Returning to teaching

Most breaks in teaching careers are taken to raise a young family. This can be a period of several years, and differs from maternity leave in that the teacher gives up her post – it will not be held open in the hope of her eventual return some years in the future. Many of those returning to teaching after a family break never really intended to do so, but make the decision because of changing circumstances.

In the case of a long absence due to illness, a teacher's post is kept open unless resignation is tendered. However, it is possible that a teacher may become fit enough to work again after many months or even years. A recent government proposal suggested that staff who were awarded ill-health pensions should be periodically re-evaluated and the pension withdrawn if the teacher were deemed fit enough to return to work. In this case the teacher might have to find a new job long after his/her old post had been filled.

Returning is never easy. The most common route is to take supply work at the teacher's old school or possibly in other schools in the region, and gradually ease back into the habits of teaching. This will help pay the bills while a new job is sought and allow a rusty teacher to regain his/her old skills. It is possible that the teacher may like working like this and never seek a permanent post, but most eventually find employment, depriving their old school of a useful source of casual cover.

Many colleges offer refresher courses for those who have been out of teaching for some years. It may also be possible to contact a local school and arrange to come in for a few days as a classroom assistant. Many primary and infant schools have nursery nurses, parents and other non-teaching staff in the classroom helping out. The presence of a fully-qualified teacher, however out of practice, is unlikely to be refused – especially if their services come free!

The situation is a little different in secondary schools, which generally have fewer outsiders in the classroom. However, arrangements can be made. I myself was invited to keep my hand in at my old teaching practice school while I was seeking a post after qualifying. The extra experience so gained might have been the deciding factor when I was approaching prospective employers. It certainly did no harm to work alongside an excellent classroom teacher for a few hours every now and then, and the motivation implied by such an arrangement looks good on the CV.

Registering as a supply teacher

As remarked elsewhere, supply teachers are not employed by schools. They are engaged for a short period from a pool of staff made available by an LEA or one of the new agencies. The school pays the LEA or agency, which in turn pays the teacher.

In order to work, then, it is necessary to register with one or more 'parent bodies'. It makes sense to register with as many as possible in order to hedge one's bets. Teachers who offer their services direct to schools without registering, as happens once in a while, are bound to run into payment problems. If they have not gone through the registration process, there is no guarantee that they are suitable for teaching work at all. This problem does not arise when the teacher is contacted through an agency or an LEA which has a supply coordinator to approach suitable staff on behalf of the school. While very rare, it occasionally happens that an unqualified person – sometimes an over-zealous student teacher seeking to improve his/her income or gain a little more experience – offers his/her services to a school. Slightly more commonly, a qualified but unregistered person offers to fill a vacancy, sometimes by accident, for example where the teacher is registered with a neighbouring LEA and does not realise that the school in question lies outside their patch. The latter case causes a few problems with payment, which might take some sorting out. To employ an unqualified supply teacher is quite simply illegal.

The LEA supply pool

Traditionally, all supply work was done through the LEA pool, a list of teaching staff registered with the appropriate local education authority. Each local authority had its own pool, and it was necessary to be registered with the LEA in the area where one intended to work. LEA pools still operate in most areas.

Registering is accomplished by requesting an application form from the local authority and returning it as if applying for any other teaching post. Instead of naming a particular post, the prospective supply teacher specifies 'Supply Pool'.

Many LEAs do not interview supply teachers, but simply conduct the appropriate security checks and inform the supply teacher than he/she is now registered. Most LEAs require at least one year's post-qualification experience, even after the demise of the Probationary Year. This is perhaps on the assumption that a teacher who has held a permanent post must have passed an interview, and there is therefore no need to conduct one, and that the year's experience is sufficient to make a teacher fit for supply work, an assumption that is certainly questionable.

Once registered, it is normally up to the supply teacher to find work for him/herself. Generally this is done by writing to local schools offering one's services, or by renewing contact with schools where the teacher has previously worked. Most such schools will be very happy to contact the supply teacher whenever an appropriate vacancy occurs. A few local authorities have coordinators who try to match teachers to vacancies on behalf of schools. Most act as nothing more than registering bodies.

The LEAs pay to scale point on a pro-rata basis. This is explained in the section on Terms and Conditions.

Agencies

In recent years, many agencies have sprung up, operating in much the same way as employment or nursing agencies. The agencies operate somewhat differently to LEA pools. Most are run by ex-teachers and/or staff with employment agency experience. They are in business to make a profit where LEAs are not, and this leads to certain distinctive characteristics.

The agencies all conduct the same security checks as schools or LEA pools and in addition will interview candidates. Further, the performance of the supply teacher in the workplace is monitored by agency administrators. This rarely happens with LEA pool supply teachers.

The benefits of an agency to the harassed deputy head are obvious. Rather than make a dozen telephone calls to those old faithful retirees who may still be active, trying to find someone free to do a short-notice cover, the deputy head can place a request with the agency office and then move on to deal with the day's other crises, secure in the knowledge that a suitable supply teacher will arrive in due course. An agency which fails to deliver the promised locum will soon be out of business, so the agency will make every effort to solve the deputy's problem. The other main advantage for schools is that agencies must be particularly careful about who they send out. So they take care to select an appropriate person for each job, and to ensure that the necessary legal matters are dealt with before a teacher is offered work; if word got out that an agency was placing staff before police checks were completed, or was using, say, unqualified students, the agency's reputation would be badly damaged with a resultant effect on business. Thus market-place considerations actually encourage good practice on the part of the agencies.

Agency supply teachers are not employed by the agency, in much the same way that employment agencies do not employ the van drivers, secretaries or bricklayers they find for firms in their fields. Agency teachers do have a contract with the agency, but this is more like an author's contract of representation with his agent than a conventional contract of employment. However, this contract does bind both parties to certain legal obligations.

The agencies do not, as a rule, pay to scale point, although some pay to scale for the lower part of the scale with a fixed top rate well below the top scale point. This is a disadvantage for the more experienced supply teacher, who could command a higher daily rate through the LEA. However, they do offer advice, support and resources to supply staff. Some agencies also insure their registered teacher with a policy similar to that used by the unions. Most do not.

Generally, it is cheaper to employ a teacher through the LEA than through an agency, but the agency offers a more comprehensive service. The choice of which to use is up to the deputy head. Most schools use both agency and LEA-registered staff as circumstances dictate.

Union membership

The teaching unions differ slightly in outlook, despite the current move towards a single union. However, all the unions offer similar benefits to their members, including:

- a reduced rate for part-time members;
- legal representation;
- newsletters;
- insurance policies to cover members against accusations of negligence and suchlike
- peripheral benefits such as reduced rate motor insurance with certain companies or insurance against malicious damage to property at work.

The main reason for union membership is legal protection. A teacher who is not a union member, faced with accusations of negligence, an unfair dismissal or any other legal problem, would be entirely on their own, forced to meet legal bills from their own means. A union member not only has representatives to advise and to appoint legal advisors as necessary, but also insurance to pay for this.

CHAPTER THREE

Finding Work

Working through the LEA

As has been previously mentioned, most LEAs do not find work for supply teachers. Some hold a list of the registered teachers, detailing their areas of competence and giving a telephone number. The school's representative can then scan the list and make a direct contact with whichever teacher seems to be most suitable. While this arrangement works passably well, it is subject to several drawbacks.

For one thing, the lists can never be completely up-to-date. Since the latest list was published, some teachers on it may have found permanent work or become unavailable for other reasons; others who have recently registered for the first time or returned to the list will not be included. Telephone numbers change and of course the chosen supply teacher may simply not be at home to answer the request. The deputy head searching for a suitable locum still has to do the leg-work in order to make contact.

The list also does not tell the whole story about each supply teacher. Many supply teachers have experience outside their own specialism which might perfectly suit them to the vacancy. If additional experience is not listed, either the locum is passed over in favour of someone else, or the deputy head may simply decide that adequate cover is not available. A dry list of names and numbers does not really help the deputy head choose the *right* person for the job.

Many authorities do not publish a list at all, but simply register the teachers and leave it entirely up to each individual to find suitable employment. They generally do this either by making their availability known on a speculative basis or by applying for specific advertised appointments.

Commonly, supply teachers will approach schools where they have previously worked, perhaps in a permanent post from which they have moved on or retired, or possibly as a student on teaching practice. In such cases, it is necessary only to telephone the school, or to visit the deputy head informally. Many retirees have a network of contacts already: staff with whom they have worked in the past, who have moved on to more senior posts and who would be pleased to hear from an old colleague and could vouch for the supply teacher's reliability and professionalism. Even a colleague who has merely changed schools and not taken on any greater responsibility is a useful contact who can deliver the application and perhaps put in a good word at the same time. This also works the other way – these contacts can make known to the supply teacher the availability of assignments which might otherwise go unnoticed.

A supply teacher seeking a wider range of possible assignments may choose to approach several or many schools, with some of which he/she will have no familiarity. This can lead to a supply teacher offering his/her services but then discovering that the school is not one he/she would want to work in. It is worth doing a little preliminary research to avoid this embarrassing situation. The supply teacher should also make sure that the school is covered by the LEA pool he/she is registered with.

Having decided to offer one's services, it is necessary to make a cold call to the school. A polite letter addressed to the person in charge of supply arrangements is most appropriate. This is usually a deputy head, as most heads delegate cover arrangements and need not be bothered with applications for casual teaching work. This letter should contain the sort of information normally carried in an application: qualifications, experience, previous appointments etc. The letter must also spell out what the prospective supply teacher can offer the school. As well as subject specialisms, the letter should explain what other subjects the teacher has taught, and should state how flexible the teacher is willing to be. Cover arrangements often require a 'mostly this but some of that' approach, which may or may not be suitable. Lastly, the letter should spell out how much notice the teacher needs; whether they are willing to take only long/short jobs or any assignment offered; any special arrangements which might have to be made, and any problems which might occur, such as how much work the teacher can accept before pension abatement rears its head.

Once the school has accepted the teacher as part of the supply team, or at least decided to give him/her a try, then the deputy head will need a telephone number where the teacher can be contacted.

The other way of finding work is more formal. In the case of small shortfalls in the school's teaching staff, maternity leave, and other similar circumstances, some schools choose to advertise. Prospective supply staff are invited to apply for the post. In the case of, say, a one-morning shortfall in the maths department, a temporary contract might be issued, but more likely the vacancy will be filled using a supply teacher. In this case the prospective supply teacher must apply as if attempting to gain a permanent post, with application letters and forms going direct to the LEA's offices, since these posts are generally paid for by the LEA rather than coming from the school's funds.

Sometimes a contract is offered in the case of maternity leave, even though the teacher is on supply and is still paid in the normal way through the LEA. In many cases there is no contract, just the usual supply agreement. In the latter case it is possible for the school or the teacher to terminate the assignment at any time without notice and with no repercussions beyond those normally expected if a teacher pulls out of a job and then attempts to return to the same school.

These advertised formal assignments account for only a very small proportion of the available supply work. Those who rely upon advertised appointments are unlikely to find as much work as they want. Similarly, it is difficult for schools to find replacement staff in a hurry. Most deputies keep a list of available supply teachers but this list constantly changes as some become unavailable, find other work, or settle down to full retirement. It is well worth helping to keep this list up-to-date by writing or calling once in a while to make sure that one has not been forgotten or lost along with the rest of the list. A deputy who cannot find one's number on that critical Tuesday morning does not have time to look for it. It is thus only sensible to make sure that he/she does not have to.

Finding work through an agency

The situation is somewhat different in the case of agency teachers, who may well also be registered with the LEA and accept work privately subject to the terms of the Agency contract. This is discussed in the chapter entitled Terms and Conditions.

Agencies exist to place supply teachers in schools. This is their function and their role. An agency which fails to do so is out of business, since its only income comes from the revenue generated by these placed teachers. So, can the teacher who has registered with an agency sit back, relax, and wait for the telephone to start ringing?

No.

The only reason an agency will accept a teacher who comes in to register is if they are a saleable asset. In other words, at the application and interview stages the agency staff will have satisfied themselves that the prospective supply teacher is capable of doing a reasonable job and not embarrassing the agency. The acid test is to see how this person performs in the field, so the new supply teacher can expect at least a couple of short assignments on a trial basis, though these will not be advertised as such, nor are they make-work. These assignments will be genuine teaching jobs.

What then? That depends entirely upon how the teacher performs. The agencies will try out anyone they think is good enough to do the job, and will almost certainly give them a second chance if things go badly. If, however, the teacher's performance is poor, lacklustre or unreliable, then they will be consigned to the also-ran collection at the bottom of the pile. There are other ways to get to the bottom of the list, too.

There is a surprisingly common misconception that the agencies operate a strict rota system, with staff sent out as they reach the top of the list for their specialism. Not only is such a system unworkable, but any thought given to the commercial side of the agency business will quickly show that a firm could not effectively operate in this fashion.

In fact, all agency supply staff are monitored, with feedback from schools actively sought, at least during the early assignments. In order to survive, the agency requires schools to want its services, i.e. those of the excellent teachers on its books. If a teacher performs badly then this reflects upon the agency, too. The deputy head might choose to look elsewhere next time. Conversely, an excellent supply teacher sitting idly at home while his/her place is taken by a poorer performer may well decide to register with another agency, losing the company a valuable asset. Neither situation is desirable.

So feedback is sought, records are carefully kept, and the agency's administrators decide who is sent out, where to, and when. These decisions are based upon the administrators' assessments of each of their registered supply teachers. Whether it exists in the form of vague ideas in an administrator's head or a formal listing on a computer system, a hierarchy exists. It is a ranking system, which dictates which of two equally qualified teachers is offered a particular assignment first. This unwritten hierachy can be manipulated.

Manipulating the hierachy

To understand the workings of the hierarchy, it is necessary to look at the process which occurs when a vacancy is filled by the agency. The type of teacher required by the school must be decided; if the school needs a specialist to teach three languages, this narrows the field dramatically as there are few such talented individuals. This vacancy would be offered to the most suitable – in the agency administrator's eyes – of the available specialists, moving down the list as necessary.

In other cases, no appropriate specialist may be available, or the school may have a policy of requesting simply a 'good all-rounder', acknowledging that sometimes it is better to have a non-specialist who can keep good order in a classroom and make a creditable effort at the work set than a genius who cannot control challenging pupils. Or the school's actual need may be vague.

Many assignments are very short-term, requiring that three or more specialisms be covered in the space of two days, and having to be filled at extremely short notice. In these cases the teacher selected for the assignment will be chosen for flexibility and reliability rather than (or as well as?) subject brilliance. The unspoken hierarchy will throw up good candidates for this kind of assignment just like any other.

The question of who is most suitable for any particular task is often difficult to answer, and it is here that the hierarchy comes into play. This hierarchy is no more than the agency's ranking of their teachers' relative abilities. It causes the administrator to select one teacher over another, time after time. Position on the hierarchy dictates how much work the supply teacher gets.

It can thus be seen that getting work through the agency involves more than just waiting for a call. If more than occasional assignments are desired, then it is a matter of climbing the hierarchy and placing oneself at the top of the list of one's specialism.

How is this done?

One can vastly increase the amount of work one is offered by the agency, by gaining a good reputation for:

- reliability;
- flexibility;
- subject brilliance;
- willingness to take on tough assignments;
- willingness to work at very short notice.

But the hierarchy is affected by other factors. These can be used to the supply teacher's advantage:

- contact – don't badger, but stay in touch. Visit the office. Become a 'face', not a 'name';
- involvement – if the agency has an event, attend it. Be noticed. Go to end-of-term parties, even just for a few minutes;
- update – if you do something good, make sure the office hears about it;
- generally try to seem keen and act as if you're interested, not burned-out and jaded.

Is it really so surprising that the agencies have their 'favourites' and 'reliables'? These are the few who always seem to be working, even in the slack times. They are the ones offered the important jobs like being the first agency teacher into a new school, or going in to salvage when someone else has messed up the assignment and the agency needs to improve its image. These are the people who make a good living out of supply. If you want to be among them, observe the above points.

But most of all, the best way of climbing the hierarchy is to be an effective supply teacher.

It is also possible to avoid the agency hierarchy altogether. Deputy heads have a hierarchy too. Whether deciding which of the old faithfuls to ring or telephoning an agency office, the deputy head already has an idea of who he/she wants to do the job. The very best way of ensuring that one finds enough work, whether through an agency or otherwise, is to make sure that one is asked for by name every time.

Besides, it's good for the ego!

CHAPTER FOUR

Expectations

In order for the temporary teacher to perform well, it is necessary to appreciate what the school as an entity and the staff as individuals might expect of him or her. These expectations are based on the school's previous experiences of supply teachers, and what it is hoping for from the next supply teacher.

Circumstances vary, as will requirements, but what follows is a description of typical expectations based upon research carried out in a large number of schools.

It is fair to say that a school will use particular temporary staff repeatedly and will request a supply teacher by name if satisfied with his/her performance. Similarly, temporary teachers may well turn down offers of work if they dislike the school, its staff or its pupils. But how does the locum impress a particular deputy head? What makes a supply teacher choose to return to a school? What motivates a supply teacher to put in the extra work, going beyond simple child-minding and actually making a teaching input into the school?

To answer these questions it is necessary to look at the expectations of the parties involved. If these expectations are met or exceeded, then the resulting good working relationship makes for a harmonious partnership which may well be repeated whenever the school needs a locum. If these expectations are not met, then one or both of the parties will be dissatisfied and this kind of partnership fails to materialise. There are no simple, hard-and-fast answers, but an appreciation of what is generally expected by both sides is a useful starting point.

The school's expectations

In the case of a temporary contract, the teacher is joining a school on a full-time basis for the duration of the contract, and is expected to function as a full member of staff from day one. The rights, duties and status of such a teacher are very similar to those of a teacher employed on a permanent contract, with the obvious exception that the term of service is finite.

The supply teacher, on the other hand, is joining a school for a period which may be as short as half a day. The status of supply teachers is therefore somewhat nebulous. Anyone who does not know what is expected of them is in for a difficult time trying to impress their temporary employer. Fortunately there is enough commonality to make at least an educated guess at what a particular school's expectations might be.

The starting point for determining a school's expectations must be the reason why the supply teacher's presence has been requested. Schools require supply cover for staff who are:

- away on training, school trips or school business;
- sick – with short- or long-term illness;
- on maternity leave;
- in school but off timetable for administrative or other reasons.

It is a general rule that the first two days of an absence due to illness are covered internally, though current union proposals seek to reduce this to a single day. Outside cover is sought after this period.

Whatever the reason, there is always some disruption caused by a teacher not being available to teach his/her own classes. This is a relatively minor problem if the teacher's absence was anticipated, or if he/she is in school and can brief the supply teacher personally. In the case of unexpected absence, the disruption is far greater. The school may find out five minutes before lessons are due to start that cover is needed, with no work set and no information available to the absent teacher's department as to what was to be done in the lessons. It is in this situation that most problems occur. Fortunately these problems can be minimised by a competent locum, often to the intense relief of the harassed deputy head.

The school will obviously expect a supply teacher to arrive in good time – or as soon as possible, if the request comes at extremely short notice. Even if the supply teacher is familiar with the school and knows that registration does not end until 9.20, the school will be more impressed with a locum who arrives at 8.45 than one who ambles in at 9.19. No matter how experienced the teacher, some period of induction and briefing is necessary, and time should be allowed for preparation. Many schools expect supply staff to mark a register, accompany pupils to assembly or perform other routine duties during the registration period. The supply teacher should be at the school in time to do this.

On arrival, the supply teacher is expected to announce him/herself. This generally means first visiting the office and obtaining a security pass if appropriate. The office may have instructions for the locum, and it is certainly unfair to make the deputy head search for the supply teacher. For this reason it is far better to ask at school reception for directions to the deputy head's office than to head straight for the staffroom for a quick cup of coffee.

Most schools expect a supply teacher to accept deviations from the planned timetable with good grace. If a teacher is requested with a view to covering geography, and arrives to find that half the day's timetable is in fact Spanish, then any reasonable school will not expect the teacher to perform wonders of linguistic ability. What is expected is that the supply teacher will not grumble and will make at least a creditable effort at the work set.

No school has the right to expect brilliance during a cover if, say, a 65-year-old retiree comes in to teach mathematics and is given football instead! Every school has the right to ask a teacher to do his or her best at whatever is necessary – within reason. This last point is discussed further below.

The school should have either a few minutes set aside for induction of supply staff or a leaflet available for their guidance. The amount of induction a supply teacher requires is obviously dependent upon several factors:

- projected length of the cover period;
- whether the school expects teaching or childminding duties from the teacher;
- whether the need for cover is more or less chaotic.

If a school is in turmoil due to multiple absences then a certain amount of coping is expected from all staff, including supply. I have myself on one occasion been responsible for the induction of other supply staff, when a school with 45 regular staff had no less than a third of its complement replaced by locums on one particular day. There was simply no time for the desperate deputy head to induct what was referred to as a 'plague of locums', so, having been at the school for a few days, I was given the task. This sort of compromise is just part of the chaos factor which attends much, though not of course all, of supply teaching. If a supply teacher cannot cope with the dislocation which goes with their occupation, they should find another job.

The school has the right to expect the supply teacher to do a certain amount of coping on his/her own. This means that during any induction period the teacher should go about finding out who they need to see about work and what the school support system is in the case of problems. The school will expect the locum to be familiar with the content of any materials given out and to display initiative as necessary. The locum teacher can reasonably be expected to familiarise him/herself with work set or to set some if there is none; to make known beforehand any problems with particular work or classes; and to liaise with the departmental head as necessary.

Perhaps most importantly, the school has the right to expect the locum to behave in a professional manner, to deal with their own classroom management as far as possible, and not to interrupt the work of other teachers and pupils unless absolutely necessary.

Some schools expect supply staff to go into a room and close the door. If no problems come through that door, then the supply teacher has succeeded, no matter what went on inside the room. This policy of accepting any sort of disruptive behaviour, so long as this does not disturb the rest of the school, is not a good thing. Pupils who get away with something with one teacher invariably have to be shown that they cannot do it with others, and this erodes the credibility of the staff as a whole in the eyes of the pupils. However demanding the alternatives may be, it is simply not professional of the school to take this attitude, although many do. Furthermore, the effect on the supply teacher who has to endure this sort of cover is not beneficial.

Other schools, commendably, expect the supply teacher to ask for help if it is needed, and will give it if requested. This approach is better for the pupils, the school and the profession (as well as the sanity of the embattled supply teacher), but it is really up to the locum to determine which approach the school prefers, and to act accordingly.

The school will expect the locum to follow school policies and to 'fit in' with the school. This means that an unorthodox or flamboyant teacher, perhaps with unusual ideas (good or bad) may have to tone down his or her approach in order to fit in with a particular school's expectations.

The school has the right to expect that staff do not cause more problems than they solve. Thus, ignoring a school policy against eating in class, or fostering the attitude in pupils that they do not have to do as they are told unless they want to, will not go down well. If staff are expected not to carry cups of coffee around the corridors during breaks, then the supply teacher should conform.

Supply teachers should know their place. They are useful professional colleagues with an important job to do – nothing more and nothing less. It is certainly not their function to constantly demand the attention of colleagues who are busy enough already.

At the end of the assignment, however long or short, the school has the right to expect the locum teacher to hand classes back without undue disruption. Even if the long-term sick colleague comes back unexpectedly, cutting short an enjoyable assignment which would have paid off the credit card bill if only it had lasted as long as originally expected, the supply teacher must still retire with good grace.

The supply teacher will often be expected to make written notes on work covered, mark books if necessary and practical, note any problems or commendations, adding any other thoughts which might be useful to the returning colleague. Such records should be passed to the department head or left where they can easily be found. There is usually a last debriefing session with the department head or deputy head, a few polite words of goodbye, then on to the next assignment!

From the school's point of view, the ideal supply teacher:

- is flexible enough to cope with unexpected changes to the assignment;
- is willing to put some initiative and effort into teaching, rather than merely childminding;
- is willing to teach creatively even outside his/her own subject area;
- can handle classroom discipline and management up to a reasonable point, and then uses the correct support procedure;
- leaves behind coherent and usable notes for the returning colleague.

Such people are godsends to the harassed deputy head who needs a cover for Mrs. Brown's classes for today, and maybe tomorrow, maybe all next week and – 'how's the diary for next month, just in case?' The school will not expect supply teachers to be miracle-workers, but if they can live up to at least some of the above expectations then they should never be short of work.

The expectations of individuals in the school

What exactly do individual members of the school community want from a supply teacher? The following reflect comments made to me during my research for this book. They are composite statements rather than direct quotations, and reflect common attitudes among those most affected by a supply teacher's work.

The deputy head's expectations

- Disciplinarians – people who can handle their classes without disrupting the rest of the school. Better that they ask for help than let something really big blow up, but better still if they can cope on their own.
- Flexibility – we often have to ask supply staff to teach outside their specialism. Things change fast around 8.30 a.m. If there's a gap in the cover timetable then we use the supply teacher to fill it; staff would be up in arms if we left the supply teacher free and asked regulars to cover instead, and besides, supply cover is expensive so we want our money's worth. If it's a reasonable request, we don't expect the supply to complain about it.
- Cooperation – we'll give the supply a free period if there's one in the absent colleague's timetable. But we do expect a similar courtesy in return, i.e. a good job during the contact periods.
- Anybody who brings a morning paper is trouble. It means they've brought something to do while they sit with classes. What do these people think they're here for? Anybody who's trying to do a good job won't be short of things to do! We don't use people like that again.
- Professionalism, both as a teacher and as a supply. There's a difference, and many locums don't appreciate that. Writing down what you did is part of the assignment.

The department head's expectations

- Competence – I'm really impressed with anyone who's willing to do practical work, so long as they're qualified to supervise it. It's better for the pupils if they can carry on with the normal syllabus. Most kids can spot 'make-work' a mile off, and they don't like their time wasted. If a supply has the subject knowledge to put something into a lesson, or even better, if they're a specialist skilled enough to pick something up in the middle, then that's the best I can ask for.

31

- Honesty – I'd rather be told that the supply has a problem or isn't happy about a piece of work before the lesson. Maybe I can do something about it then. Halfway through is a little late.

The colleague's expectations

- I don't mind someone popping into my classroom to ask me for advice or whatever, or if they can put a disruptive pupil in my room for a bit. That's part of the job. I do object to endless interruptions, whether it's a noisy class or the teacher in person. I've got a job to do, too.
- I hate to see someone who's getting paid more than I am, and on a pension too in some cases, doing nothing while the kids tear the furnishings to pieces. And people who take up three chairs in the staffroom, including mine, with their stuff, yet say nothing pleasant to anyone all day!
- Supply teachers are getting younger. That's not good or bad really. There were good and bad retirees doing the job, and now there are good and bad 25-year-olds doing it. Many of the younger teachers are inexperienced and they make mistakes – but most of them try very hard to do a good job. Maybe that's because they haven't got cynical about it yet, or maybe they really want to learn. I can forgive mistakes if the supply is genuinely trying to do a good job. But I do expect to see them trying – all of them, however young or old.
- I expect them to be pleasant and courteous. This is *our* staffroom, and they're guests as well as colleagues. I'm always friendly to new faces and I expect the same in return.
- I expect them not to make more work for me than the person they're replacing!

The school secretary's expectations

- I normally expect a retiree, but more and more young people are coming through, gaining experience or paying the bills until they find a permanent job. I hate people who come here just to earn some money. That's not what teaching's about. I expect people coming in in the morning to arrive with a good attitude. It doesn't matter who they are as long as they're qualified, competent and willing to do a job of work.

- I don't expect to have to chase up registers, keys and suchlike. Supply staff are always forgetting things like that and it's very annoying.

The pupil's expectations

- Don't like the disruption. I really hate the pointless work that's just set to keep us quiet. If there's a point to it, fair enough, but if not . . .
- They don't know who's who. You can go in the wrong classes and sit with your mates. If you run off in the corridor they can't identify you. They're fun to mess about. It's a real shock if you get one that's willing to follow his threats up!
- They're too strict. Always trying to 'make their mark'. They go off it for nothing, just to look tough. If they were reasonable with you it'd work better, but it's like they've got to look tougher than normal teachers.
- There're too soft, like they can't be bothered.
- The best ones do something different and unusual. It's a break from routine, especially if they're nice.
- What's the difference? Teachers are teachers. They're all the same so why worry about it? Supply teachers are no different to others. What's the difference anyway?

Overall expectations within the school

It can be seen from the last section that pupils' expectations vary widely, as might be expected. With a few exceptions, staff expectations are surprisingly similar from school to school. It follows that a school and its staff will not be impressed with a teacher who fails to live up to expectations or who lives up to the negative ones, while the most important factor is a willingness to put some effort into the supply assignment – in short, not to be merely qualified cover, someone with Qualified Teacher Status to be wheeled into the classroom at nine and out again at four, but a supply *teacher*. Such a person regards the assignment as his or her job, and goes into the classroom with the expectation of teaching, not childminding.

There are no prizes for guessing which type of supply teacher is persistently requested by schools, nor which names stay at the top of agency lists.

The supply teacher's expectations

Many teachers are unsure what they can reasonably expect from the school, and for this reason some are hesitant about asking for information or other assistance to which they are in fact entitled. Similarly, some schools will ask rather more of the locum teacher than is strictly correct. This is not always deliberate, and a teacher has the right to query any request. The problem lies in identifying exactly what is reasonable and what is not. So what does a locum teacher have the right to expect?

Firstly, every locum may expect the same courtesy and consideration offered to regular staff. An attitude that 'you're only a supply' on the part of the school is counterproductive, as is treating temporary staff as dogsbodies, coffee-makers and second-class citizens. The result is poor motivation and a resulting lacklustre performance. Of course, some schools show their own staff very little consideration. In this situation the supply teacher may be in the same boat as everyone else, but fortunately this is rare.

Arriving at the school, the locum teacher should expect a suitable induction. This is most likely to be rather sketchy in the case of a one-day cover, but certain basic requirements exist, whether the teacher is required for a morning or a term. There is sometimes no way of knowing whether or not a single-day cover might suddenly become a long-term assignment. In such cases a good induction at the start can save problems later on. Induction is discussed at greater length in Chapter Five.

The supply teacher expects to have the same access to coffee machines, kettles, canteens and other vital life-support machinery as other staff, and also the same access to teaching and learning resources. Especially important can be the assistance of technicians where they are available. Technicians are often in an excellent position to assist newcomers to the school when other teachers are busy with classes. This situation should not be misused; technicians have their own extremely important jobs to do, and are there to support the department rather than any one member of it.

The supply teacher has the same rights to security and support as any other member of staff. Ideally, the supply teacher should be thought of by the school as simply another member of staff, and treated accordingly. This cuts both ways: if regular staff are expected to perform dinner duties or see pupils off the site at the end of the school day then supply staff should expect to be asked to do so too. In return the supply teacher should expect timely notice of changes to the timetable, unusual situations or pupils who need special attention. There is no excuse for a school placing a supply teacher in charge of a violent pupil or one with a serious medical condition without at least making the teacher aware of the situation.

If the assignment goes on longer than originally planned, as often happens when a member of staff is long-term absent, then the supply teacher can expect to be kept up to date with the situation. If the absentee has just put in another month's sick note, the supply teacher should expect to be told about it. Sometimes it is necessary to ask, since senior staff are busy with a variety of tasks, but the information should be available.

It is necessary always to balance what is desirable against what is possible in a given set of circumstances. Every school has its own way of treating temporary staff, and the supply teacher has no reason to expect the school to change its policies. For example, some schools believe that a supply teacher should put in a full day even if the teacher they are covering for has free periods. After all, the supply teacher has less administrative work to do. The locum's timetable will be filled up with odd bits and pieces from the cover list to give the regular staff some relief. This is reasonable, since the supply teacher is being paid for a full day's work. Other schools will give the supply teacher free time if it is on the absent colleague's timetable. Neither approach is necessarily right or wrong, but it is reasonable to expect a supply teacher to use free time productively, to mark work or write an account of topics covered. The school should make this clear at the outset.

Supply teachers must decide for themselves whether the demands being made on them are reasonable or not, but a locum has the right to refuse certain duties, just as any member of the profession does. For example, specialist training is required before a teacher is eligible for cover under the school's insurance for physical education or practical work in science or technology. This includes food technology and textiles, a fact overlooked by some staff and schools; domestic experience is not considered adequate training to teach these subjects. If asked to cover practical lessons the teacher who lacks the requisite qualifications has the right – indeed the duty – to refuse.

It is up to the locum to decide what to do in any given circumstance. For example, if asked to cover a PE lesson where two classes are placed together, in company with an experienced and qualified PE teacher, the supply teacher should be adequately covered since he/she is functioning as an assistant rather than being in charge of the class. But in the case of a history teacher being asked to sit in on a science practical lesson, the situation is definitely outside the teacher's competence and thus illegal. This request should be refused.

There are many grey areas, for example harmless practicals like measuring the pH of rainwater, and teachers must use their judgement in every case, bearing in mind that 'it seemed safe enough' is not a legal defence if some bizarre accident does occur. The supply teacher has the right, indeed the legal obligation, to query any request which causes doubt and to refuse such requests if necessary.

In short, it is reasonable to expect a supply teacher to cover subjects outside his or her field, in the same way that a regular member of staff might be so asked. It is not reasonable to ask supply teachers to place themselves at risk covering practical subjects beyond their competence. Honesty and assertiveness on the part of the locum are required in this case.

Finally, the supply teacher has the right to leave an assignment. If the cover is of several weeks' duration and the locum discovers that he or she does not wish or is unable to continue, he/she has the right to terminate the assignment, This is not likely to please a harassed deputy head or agency administrator, but the right to vote with one's feet should be borne in mind.

Some schools have trouble keeping temporary staff, whether through staff or pupil problems. I have watched a succession of supply staff arrive to fill the same long-term cover, stay a day (or less) and then leave, never to return. In some schools this is the norm, and the supply teacher has the right to turn down or terminate an assignment for the sake of his/her own sanity. It is not, however, a decision to be taken lightly. A reputation for being flighty or unreliable will be hard to shake off.

In short, then, the supply teacher has the right to a suitable induction, to personal security and support, and to leave the assignment at any time. He/she also has the right to negotiate his/her duties with the school and to come to a workable compromise.

Most important of all, a supply teacher has the right to respect and treatment similar to that accorded any fellow professional. Supply teachers are expected to function as teachers, and they have the right to be treated as such.

CHAPTER FIVE
Induction

Approaches to induction

There are two approaches commonly applied to the induction of supply staff: a personal introduction and a handout. Most schools use one or both to some degree. Those schools which are not really interested in supply teacher performance do neither, and reap their just rewards in good time. From the supply teacher's perspective, the very best schools to work in use both approaches, and thoroughly.

The personal introduction

The supply teacher is met at school reception or told how to find the person in charge of supply cover. In the case where that person is busy with other business, an apology for changed circumstances is offered and an alternative arrangement made.

It is entirely reasonable for a deputy head to attend to an internal crisis, leaving the supply teacher sitting about in reception if necessary. It is not, however, reasonable to expect a supply teacher to find his or her way about an unfamiliar school, searching the corridors for someone, anyone, who can tell them what they are supposed to be doing. Any school with decent security will quickly eject such wanderers, which can be somewhat embarrassing for all concerned.

Once the person in charge of supply is available, the supply teacher is given a quick tour of the site. The content of this tour should be as follows:

- The supply teacher is shown to his/her classroom, given a timetable and introduced to relevant personnel such as department heads and colleagues who have neighbouring classrooms. Generally one of these persons will be nominated to assist the supply teacher with any queries as necessary.
- The supply teacher is shown other important areas such as toilets, staffroom, canteens. He/she is told who to see about time sheets and other administrative matters at the end of the day.
- Procedures are spelled out to the supply teacher: registers, discipline, marking, locations of equipment etc. Any queries the locum may have can be addressed at this point.
- The supply teacher is then left to organise him/herself and the classroom, to look over the work to be covered, and to generally prepare for the arrival of the pupils.

Having been given this kind of introduction, it is wise to make notes as there is really no excuse for forgetting what one has been told.

The handout

Any school which does not have a prepared handout for supply teachers is wasting its own time.

The teacher is bound to have queries throughout the day. Unable to refer to a handout, the confused locum will either take a best guess and possibly make a mistake, or else go in search of a colleague to ask. This interrupts lessons with the usual consequences for pupil concentration. Similarly, pupils who are inclined to be difficult will realise that a supply teacher is unsure of procedures, and will take full advantage. It is sometimes only necessary to hint that, for example, a duty teacher might be called to remove a difficult pupil in order to defuse the situation. The teacher in this case has shown that he or she knows what to do. The difficult pupils will often subside upon realising that they are not going to get away with anything. And if not, well at least the supply teacher knows what to do about it.

Some schools go so far as to give locum staff a copy of the staff handbook. This is excellent for longer-term assignments and temporary contracts, but I know from experience the joys of carrying a 60-page ring binder around the school and trying to wade though it in odd moments during the day. Large documents like this are really too big to be useful. A shorter handout is desirable, with only essential information contained within. A teacher on a one-day cover has not time for anything more.

A handout given in conjunction with a tour and personal introductions is a sign of a well organised school which is prepared to support temporary staff. Such a school will want something in return, i.e. effort on the part of the locum, but has already gone a long way towards motivating the supply teacher to do a good job.

A teacher given both a handout and a personal introduction should give solemn thanks at a suitable opportunity. Not only is this approach the most effective, it is also evidence of an excellent attitude towards supply staff.

Induction sheet contents

Induction documents differ from school to school, but the overall content should contain most or all of the following:

1. **A map of the school site.** This should be clearly marked and readable. It need not be complex, nor up to OS standards, so long as the average person can find their way around with it. Bad photocopies are more confusing than helpful.

2. **Lesson Times.** A favourite dodge of certain types of pupil is the old 'you can't hear the bell in here . . . we finish at five past' routine. Even good classes will try this one if they think they can get away with it. This can cause embarrassment if the supply teacher falls for it. A copy of lesson times (and a watch, obviously) is thus most useful.

3. **Access.** Where to obtain keys, or who to contact to open classrooms. The handout should state whether keys can be sent with pupils or must be returned personally.

4. **Administration.** Who to see about timesheets etc.

5. **A list of all staff.** Or at least the senior staff, and where they can be contacted (room numbers, extensions). This is useful for a variety of purposes, from getting hold of assistance if needed, to sending a pupil to ask for rulers, keys or worksheets.

6. **A code of conduct for staff.** Guidelines on such issues as smoking (where it is allowed and where not), on requirements for outside duties, on procedures for dealing with emergencies from pupil violence to fire, chemical spill or sudden illness.

7. **A code of conduct for pupils.** Clear statements of school rules for pupils, such as 'chewing, eating and drinking are not allowed in classrooms'. The supply teacher should be familiar with school rules and should not make exceptions.

Also, any other relevant information, such as special circumstances or considerations, is likely to be appended on a separate sheet, as and when needed.

CHAPTER SIX

Effective Supply Teaching

What to know before setting out

The phone rings. The supply teacher answers. At the other end of the line is someone – deputy head, agency coordinator or whoever – who needs a supply teacher. The request may be coming at very short notice, and the caller may have very little time to spare. Brevity is a virtue at 8.30 a.m.

Firstly, one must determine whether or not one can actually accept the assignment. The question, 'are you free to work today?' generally requires the answer, 'it depends'. Supply teachers need information at this point:

- Which school/college/other institution?
- What is to be taught/covered?
- When does the assignment begin?
- How long is it likely to last?

It is usually possible to give a firm answer based upon this information. One might be free today, but not tomorrow. A two-day assignment would therefore be impossible in this case. Some supply teachers are willing to take one-day covers while others are not. Some have commitments which must be worked around. The above four statements reflect the minimum information required to make a decision.

Other information will probably be necessary, and if the response so far is a 'yes', then the details can be filled in. A few questions at this stage can save time later. The most commonly requested information is:

- An address or directions to the school.
- What time to arrive?
- Who to report to on arrival?
- Is the school expecting a preliminary contact?
- What is the school like to work in?
- Are there any special considerations?
- Is the assignment likely to run longer than this?

Most of the above is self-explanatory, and of course unnecessary if the supply teacher has worked in this particular institution before. It is well worth making a preliminary contact if one is expected. This might be in the form of a phone call or a visit. It is almost certain to be expected in the case of a long-term cover, and almost impossible in a soon-as-possible situation.

Special considerations can be almost anything. Sometimes the school may want the supply teacher to have special equipment with him/her, for example a lab coat for science or appropriate footwear if the teacher may be using a gym – whether for PE or otherwise. Other special considerations include special needs awareness or familiarity with a particular computer system.

It may seem a little cheeky to ask a deputy head what his or her school is like to work in. After all, who is going to tell the prospective supply teacher that their institution closely resembles Bash St. School?

Actually most deputy heads will be quite truthful about the nature of their school. There is no point in recruiting a supply teacher who will wilt in the face of Class Seven Triple-X. Nobody will come out and say, 'We're a bit of a hell-hole actually,' but phrases like, 'Well, some of the pupils can be a bit . . . challenging' are sufficient warning. Forewarned is forearmed, they say. More importantly, this information gives the supply teacher a chance to consider if the assignment is really such a good idea, without letting everyone down by quitting halfway through the morning.

It is sometimes impossible to say whether an assignment may run on, but there are circumstances where it definitely will not, such as where a colleague is off timetable for a specific period for some task, e.g. exam board moderating. This is not to say that the supply teacher will not be immediately offered a different assignment in the same school, so it is wise to be prepared for this eventuality.

Some of the information above can be gained immediately, some from a preliminary call or visit. But all of it is worth having, and enables the supply teacher to make an informed decision about whether or not to take the offered assignment. Once the assignment has started, this information continues to be useful, reducing the number of questions that need to be asked upon arrival. No information is any use unless it is available, so unless you have an exceptional memory, *write it down*!

What to arrive with

Supply staff cannot be expected to provide equipment the school lacks. Indeed, most departments will have adequate supplies of pens, paper etc. handy for use during the cover lesson. How to gain access to these invaluable items will have been explained during whatever induction the supply teacher has been given.

However, the well-prepared supply teacher has a few things handy in case of shortages. Cover lessons are difficult enough without proceedings skidding to a stop because no less than seven members of a class lack pens. At the very least a pack of cheap ball-points in the supply teacher's possession can save aggravation. An A4 notepad and a couple of rulers can be useful too. Lending one's personal property to unknown children is not desirable, but the above represent tools of the trade and should be considered expendable if necessary.

Overall, the supply teacher who possesses any sense has the following in a bag by the door, to be grabbed in case of short-term cover requests:

- writing paper
- pens
- a couple of rulers
- a number of 'lesson ideas' which require minimum preparation and equipment

- pencils
- an A-Z of the area he/she normally works in
- agency time sheets if appropriate
- sports kit (possibly).

The latter is really only necessary for those who are frequently asked to cover PE. This is not exclusively the preserve of trained PE teachers, so it is worth having equipment handy, just in case.

What to ask upon arrival

Upon presenting oneself at the school office, and having identified oneself, there is a minimum of information required to be of any use to the school. This is:

- Where to find the person in charge of supply cover?
- Where to find the appropriate department head?
- Which classrooms will the supply teacher be using?
- Is work set? Where to find it?
- Where to return resources/work to?
- Is technician support available?
- Where are the toilets, staffroom and eating facilities?
- Smoking policy, if any?
- What is the school's discipline procedure?
- What is the support arrangement for major problems?

Many supply teachers are unwilling to ask about discipline, in case they imply that their own discipline is not sufficient. Yet most schools, first and foremost, want control of covered classes. In a cover situation actual teaching often comes second to not doing any damage by letting classes run wild. Unless the senior staff send very clear signals that they are not interested in what happens in your classroom, then find out about the discipline and support systems – and use them. Most staff are realists who will respect someone willing to admit the possibility of problems, who at the same time finds out how to deal with them. To quote my own first head of department: 'I don't judge new staff on how many problems they have. I judge them on how effectively they deal with those problems.'

It is likely that most of the above information will be conveyed in an induction of some kind, but these are the main points to look and listen for.

Establishing and maintaining control

Supply teaching can be a funny business. It can be like starting a string of new posts and never becoming established. It can mean starting from scratch every day. It can mean never establishing the classroom environment you want to have and going home every night convinced that you've completely lost any ability you may have once had to control pupils.

It doesn't have to be that bad, but in order to avoid problems it is necessary to grab control of the situation right from the start. The very best way to establish classroom control is to begin every assignment, even a single session, as if this were a new post you will hold for the next twenty years. Find out the school policy on discipline and work within it. Don't go overboard and give out punishments for the sake of making a name for yourself as a disciplinarian – there is no real need. But resist the temptation to let the little things go. It is quite possible that in the course of an hour's lesson a minor incident of, say, disobedience over something like chewing in class can landslide into a classroom riot.

It happens.

A large part of control is 'hidden mechanisms', subtle measures not immediately obvious to the pupils – or even to oneself. Simply appearing confident helps. A cheerful, polite but firm demeanour is important. It is easy to offend a pupil or a whole class by trying to appear too authoritarian or, worse, by being brisk, sarcastic, rude and abrasive. Offended pupils respond in kind, and you may never realise that the reason for your disaster was simply that you were irritated with the class and snapped, 'Shut up!' instead of saying, 'Let's have a bit of quiet when I'm talking, please.'

Insist on good classroom practice. Pupils will almost certainly be expected to remove outdoor coats, gloves, snowshoes etc. upon arrival. Non-uniform items such as 'logo' sweatshirts should be queried, at the very least. Find out beforehand what the policy is – and stick to it. Do not allow pupils to swing on chairs or throw scrap paper at the bin instead of walking up and putting it in – and don't do these things yourself! Trying to put a stop to what has just become accepted practice in your classroom is going to be a problem.

Try to establish a business-like atmosphere. Pupils come to school to work. They know that, even if they prefer not to admit it. So be organised, have the materials you need handy. Explain what is required in a concise manner and let them get on with it. Don't get drawn into the inevitable 'Where are you from? What's your favourite football team?' questions. Not only is there a risk that a fervent supporter of some rival team will immediately decide to resent your presence, leading to friction, but on a more mundane note it allows pupils to become legitimately distracted or over-familiar.

Don't sit down. As a rule, a seated teacher becomes invisible to pupils, and is quickly forgotten about. It is as if, by sitting at the teacher's desk, one is sending a signal to the pupils that one is not interested in what they are doing. If you're not interested then why should they be? Noise levels shoot up and require hard words to quieten. Pupils then resent the teacher's attitude, and problems snowball. Don't let it happen. Instead, move about the room as the class are working. Simply standing near a chatting pupil serves to remind most that they have a task to be working on, even if you're ostensibly examining the wall displays. If a pupil needs to be directed back on task, it is better to say, 'Any problems with that?' – they may well have, but be unwilling to attract your attention – rather than, 'Get on with your work now!'

Be subtle at first, but be firm. Ask, then tell. *Then* you can threaten to send the pupil to withdrawal or whatever the system is for refusal to obey. You know what the disobedience policy in the school is, because you asked beforehand.

Didn't you?

Don't make implausible threats unless you want to look a fool. Don't threaten violence. If you've made a (sensible) threat, and your bluff is called, carry it out. *Never* back down or compromise. 'If you have said, so must you do.'

Pupils will walk in, look at you, and start issuing invitations to their friends to 'Come and sit with me'. Despite the fact that you don't know where their normal seats are, a firm injunction to 'Sit in your own seats, please' often results in resigned obedience from the pupils. If you are suspicious that you've been ignored, watch the possible culprits and move them at the first sign of trouble; you've already given them the benefit of the doubt so don't do it again.

Don't ever let pupils rake around in cupboards or desks, whatever their ostensible reason or however plausible their explanation. Keep track of what you loan out and don't give new exercise books out to the incredible number of pupils whose books have been lost by the previous teacher, or who were promised one last lesson. Insist upon seeing the full old book before issuing a new one. It is amazing how authority evaporates as pupils realise that you have been conned again.

Hopefully, all of the above is obvious. Classroom management techniques – moving disruptive pupils and suchlike – are taught in teacher training. They apply to supply teachers too – don't forget that. Whatever pupils may say to the contrary, this is your classroom for the time being. Whatever policies Mr Calder may (or may not – pupils will make some unlikely claims) have had, you are in charge here and now. You know what time lessons change. You don't let pupils go early. You insist that coats are taken off, even if they claim they normally keep them on. Stick to the rules.

Always.

Establishing control can be difficult at the best of times, but for a teacher who does not know pupils' names, who may never be back after today, the problems are many times greater. What do you have on your side?

More than you might think.

Except in the very roughest schools, there is an assumption of authority among the pupils. Although they may challenge this assumption, they know the teacher is in charge. It is easy to lose this assumption in the face of challenge or steady erosion, but it is there to begin with.

The pupils often have very little information. Don't tell them that you are only in for the morning. Most borderline villains will err on the side of caution if they think you will be back tomorrow and there might actually be consequences to their actions.

The school has a discipline system already. If you know how it works (or look like you do), and are willing to use it, then it can work for you, too. You also have colleagues nearby who are usually willing to help out if necessary. It is not wise to abuse this goodwill for the sake of a quiet life, but the option is there if you need to ask for help.

Most schools operate some kind of 'red card' system, whereby a senior member of staff is available to attend any disturbance if necessary. This system is there to be used. Using it judiciously will not offend anyone, and pupils may be slower to transgress in future if they see you mean business.

And don't forget your own skills. You are a trained, experienced professional. Your classroom management skills can head off a great deal of potential trouble. In fact, the biggest thing you have going for you is your own considerable ability.

But why? Why bother? Why not read the paper, keep your head down and collect the money at the end of the day? Why put in all that work to maintain a discipline system that doesn't affect you? Why does it matter what happens in someone else's classroom anyway?

It is to be hoped that you already know the answers to these questions. Professional pride is one reason. Self-respect, a sense of duty to the future generations who rely on you for their education, and loyalty to the profession – these are all good reasons. A good performance may lead to more offers of work in the future, and therefore greater financial security for you. Are any of these good enough reasons to put the paper down and start teaching?

Hopefully, but if not then here's the best reason of all: the school has brought in a supply *teacher*, at considerable expense, to fill the gap in the timetable. If they wanted a child-minder they'd have hired one.

Reading the paper is not teaching.

And if you're not teaching then you're in the wrong job.

CHAPTER SEVEN
Staying On

In many cases it is all but impossible to predict how long an assignment will run for. In the case where a member of staff is off timetable for a fixed period – say a morning to attend a moderating meeting – it is fairly certain that this short cover is all that will be asked of the supply teacher. But this is not always the case. Sometimes some other need for cover will arise, and the deputy head will then turn to the nearest source of cover, the supply teacher who is already in the building, and ask 'Can you just . . . ?'

In most cases the future is even less clear. A simple two-day cover for an absent colleague may run on and on as the sick notes begin to appear at regular intervals. The supply teacher who came in for two days may well find him/herself asked back for a week, then another, then a month. If the supply teacher has a clear diary and is working within his/her specialism, then problems are unlikely. But in many cases the supply is out of place, just filling in for a couple of days. This is usually the case when the need for cover arises unexpectedly and at very short notice. The locum may be teaching well outside his/her specialism, having come in on a short-term basis since simply having a qualified person in the classroom is a necessity.

This situation is acceptable in the short term. Almost anyone can administer work set by a colleague – or set their own – for a short time without undue harm to the pupils' educational prospects. But as time goes on, the school and the supply teacher must evaluate the situation and decide what to do for the best. It might be that the supply teacher, while not a specialist in the required subject, has enough background knowledge and general teaching ability to perform adequately. Perhaps in this case swapping the adequate all-rounder for a specialist of unknown virtue may not be desirable; at least the school is familiar with the current locum's shortcomings and can compensate. Bringing in a specialist causes at least one more dislocation for pupils and staff alike, and perhaps more than one if this new specialist is not suitable, or later decides that the assignment is not appropriate.

Sometimes it is best to leave things as they are, and most deputies will not change an arrangement that seems to be working, on the off-chance that things might get even better. Many schools recognise that the disruption caused by bringing in another new teacher may far outweigh the advantages of having a specialist, and operate on a principle of 'if it ain't broke, don't fix it.'

From three days to nine months

It was the first day of the January term. Mr Jenkins had been absent for several weeks, and a supply teacher had been found to teach his maths classes until his return, hopefully during the second week of term. The supply teacher had failed to turn up due to family troubles. The harassed deputy head amended the internal cover list for the morning and rang an agency. Assured that someone would arrive by lunch-time, he then began trying to placate those who had been given the task of covering the maths classes.

The agency administrator rang every maths teacher she knew. Nobody wanted to work that day, not on the first day of term. A few had said they would only do long-term work and this was just three days . . . hardly worth it.

Finally the administrator rang Joe Brown, a chemistry teacher who might be willing to give it a go. Joe assured her that his maths was, well, adequate and that he could happily run maths lessons for three days if someone else set the work. Besides, Joe lived ten minutes from the school and time was running short. He was willing to give it a go, and that would have to do.

The administrator called the school and outlined the situation, including Joe's mathematical limitations. 'Great. Soon as possible,' responded the deputy head, who by now had other problems.

Joe turned out to be a very mediocre maths teacher, and struggled to cope in what turned out to be a fairly tough school. But he turned up every day, and tried to teach the work set by the head of department, even though this meant relearning trigonometry in the staffroom ten minutes before the lesson. Most of all, Joe worked hard to maintain the school's discipline policy and general ethos. His new colleagues liked him. He fitted in.

At the end of the week, Mr Jenkins did not return. Nor the following week, nor the one after that. Then the first of the monthly sick notes appeared. Joe was asked to visit the deputy head's office.

The deputy head asked a few questions: how was Joe getting on, was he having any problems, how did he like being a Maths teacher? Joe truthfully replied that he was struggling but getting support from his colleagues, and that he was learning a great deal about mathematics. The deputy head spelled out the situation – that it was possible that the assignment might run for months yet. After consultation with the department head, the conclusion had been reached that Joe was not a particularly good maths teacher, but he was a good *teacher*. The school had considered letting him go and bringing in a specialist now that one could be found, but felt that the disruption so caused would outweigh any advantages. The decision would thus be left to Joe: if he wanted to continue, he could have the job until Mr Jenkins came back. And if Mr Jenkins didn't come back and the post had to be advertised . . . would Joe consider applying?

Joe accepted. He remained at the school for nearly nine months, until Mr Jenkins finally came back. For his willingness to try something that required a bit of effort, and at short notice, Joe got several months' work at a time when he needed it. He didn't get the full-time post, since Mr Jenkins came back. What he did get was a great deal of very good experience and a glowing reference. Then Miss Davis from the IT department went on maternity leave. The deputy head immediately rang the agency office and asked if Joe was available . . . .

Approaching the assignment

It is obvious that circumstances change. A short assignment may run on, or a new assignment may materialise at the same school just as the locum is on the way out of the door. Many schools try out the staff who come in on supply, stating that the assignment is for 'one week initially', then extending the period if the locum proves suitable. If not, then a new supply teacher can be found for the next week, and no one has the embarrassing task of telling a locum that he/she is no use. This may seem slightly underhanded, but it happens.

It is thus well worth approaching every assignment on the assumption that it may be far longer than expected. Keeping one's head down may avoid problems with disruptive pupils for a single morning – or indeed it may not – but if the assignment is extended or one comes back another time, then those disruptive pupils will have the measure of this particular supply teacher. Having started the assignment behaving like a soft touch, it is extremely difficult to regain control.

Treating every half-day assignment like the beginning of a new permanent post is not always practicable, but will impress most deputy heads. It is better for the profession as a whole in the long run; too many pupils think that having a supply teacher equates to doing whatever they like. From the supply teacher's point of view, the approach taken on that single morning might be the deciding factor in determining whether the supply teacher is discreetly let go, or is asked to come back tomorrow. Putting in that effort at the beginning pays off when one is suddenly asked to stay on – and it may be the reason *why* one is asked to stay.

From a purely practical viewpoint, it is worth arriving at a school in the morning with the assumption that one could be staying all day, even if the assignment is just for the morning, i.e. bring something for lunch, or money to buy lunch from the school canteen; be ready to cancel the afternoon's shopping trip.

This approach is only common sense. If the assignment is extended once, it may be extended again. If the locum has to turn down that extension then it will go to someone else. It seems a shame to let work go simply owing to a lack of preparation.

If the cover period is extended beyond a few days, then the school will start wanting the supply teacher to function as part of the school, rather than as a stop-gap measure. It will become necessary to begin marking work, and perhaps take over a tutor group or outside duties. Exactly when in the assignment this transition takes place varies widely, but what should be expected is that it will happen. Once the locum has been teaching at a particular school for a few weeks, there is really no reason why he/she should not fulfil the same duties as permanent staff. This may include covering lessons in the supply teacher's free periods if he/she is lucky enough to have any.

CHAPTER EIGHT

Making a Career of Supply Teaching

At an interview with a teaching agency, I was once told, 'You understand you can't make a career of supply teaching, don't you?' A few years later, a coordinator with a different agency remarked, 'If anyone's made a career of it, it's you.'

So can one make a career in supply teaching? Yes and no.

It is quite possible to ensure that one earns enough through the teaching year to cover the holidays and to live quite comfortably. It would no doubt be possible to do this year in and year out for one's entire working life.

It's not much of a career, though. There is no development, no promotion, and relatively little job satisfaction to be had. The stress experienced by most classroom teachers is if anything worse for any locum who really cares about their job. After all, the sort of schools which regularly need long-term supply cover are generally the ones that are tougher to work in, and the locum spends a great deal of his or her working life flitting from job to job without settling in properly.

Overall, then, it *is* possible to make a career in supply, but it is perhaps a spectacularly bad idea to try! However, if one has some goal in mind, then working in supply for several years is quite acceptable. Possible reasons may include:

- gaining experience or waiting for the right job to come up;
- building some alternative career;
- family commitments;
- a lack of permanent posts;
- the traditional, post-retirement supply assignments.

In most of the above cases, the supply teacher will want to work less than full-time, and thus cannot take on a permanent post. Or it might be desirable to be able to terminate any assignment at short notice, say if one's book is published or one's business begins to take off. In the case where supply teaching is one's main, or only, job and the only prospect for the foreseeable future, then one will want as much work as possible. It becomes necessary to choose carefully between assignments in order to maximise one's income. For example, if one were offered the choice between a full week this week with no guarantees after that, or the assurance of three days a week for the next seven weeks, which is more desirable? There are many factors, but some knowledge of the patterns of work availability throughout the year might help one to choose wisely.

The teaching year

Generally speaking, the distribution of available work throughout the year is more uniform in primary schools than secondary, and there are sudden fluctuations in both which defy the trends, but the following overall pattern has emerged.

There is very little work available in September. The situation improves a little as the term goes on, but there are generally fewer staff absent due to illness in the first half of the autumn term. The summer's rest helps hold stress and illness at bay until half-term. After the half-term, winter illnesses begin to take their toll and work picks up considerably. This is true through the January term – the second term of the year is the 'best' for supply teachers. As the weather warms up, illnesses become fewer and in secondary schools once the Year 11 pupils have left more internal cover becomes available, so fewer supply staff are needed.

Long-term illness, maternity leave and odd days for meetings, trips and other off-timetable activities occur more or less evenly throughout the year.

Pensions and benefits

Teachers who register with an agency are generally required to opt out of the Teachers' Superannuation Scheme. The agency makes automatic deductions for tax and National Insurance contributions, but makes no provision for holidays, for sick pay or any form of pension or retirement benefit. On the plus side, this opting out means that a retiree working through an agency can earn as much as he/she likes without suffering any form of pension abatement.

The supply teacher (LEA or agency) is of course entitled to statutory benefits such as Statutory Sick Pay or Jobseeker's Allowance. However, this is subject to having made sufficient National Insurance contributions in the preceding years. Since a supply teacher cannot by definition work during the school holidays, something must be done about these contributions. It is quite possible to have paid considerable amounts in NI contributions for several years, say after working full-time for 30 weeks of the year. The amount paid is more than enough to qualify the supply teacher for benefits through the summer holidays or a period of illness – but despite having paid a large amount, the teacher does not qualify.

The reason for this is that there is a requirement to have made at least a minimum contribution each week, including those weeks where the teacher cannot work. To bring contributions up to date, it is possible to contact the DSS and find out how much the missing contributions add up to, then pay it as a lump sum. To keep current contributions up to date, one can make a payment for each week for which there is no automatic contribution made by the agency. Failure to keep up to date results in the teacher becoming ineligible for any benefits and also losing that year's contributions towards a state pension.

Whether National Insurance contributions are kept up to date or not, the supply teacher would be wise to seek advice on a private pension scheme since, having opted out of the Teachers' Superannuation Scheme, there is no provision for anything beyond the state pension. This has equal relevance to agency and LEA supply teachers, though those already on a pension need not worry.

Choosing between assignments and rejecting unsuitable offers

It is sometimes the case that a teacher working through more than one agency, or who is associated with several schools, may be offered several assignments at much the same time. One has to weigh the benefits and take a realistic approach in this case. If the supply teacher has just agreed to do a single day in the coming week, then is called by a different school wanting a locum full-time for the next six months, the choice seems obvious. Bearing in mind that the supply teacher must make a living, the realistic choice must be to take the longer assignment, taking care to let down the original school as lightly as possible. But what of the case where a teacher is offered, say, three days in the coming week then receives an offer of a whole week elsewhere? The situation is somewhat different. While no reasonable person will expect the supply teacher to impoverish him/herself for the sake of honouring an agreement, the locum who makes a habit of cancelling jobs will notice a sharp reduction in the availability of work.

There are several schools in which I refuse to work. Any offers are politely turned down. Every supply teacher has the right to do this, and turning down one job should not prejudice an agency against offering others in the future. However, one must take care not to build a reputation for refusing work. A good reason should be offered in the case of offers coming through an agency.

'Not today; it's raining,' is not a good reason, though, believe it or not, agencies have heard it.

'I've worked there before, and frankly the school is a dump and the pupils are, well, challenging. Sorry, but I just don't want to work there,' is quite legitimate, if rather more forthright than polite. However, it is the supply teacher's decision whether or not to accept an offer of work, and so long as an adequate reason is offered there should be no harm to a teacher's reputation. There is no reason to tell lies, and in the end it is counterproductive anyway.

It does not pay to turn down too many offers, and at certain times of the year the tough schools might be the only ones needing cover. To work or not to work? The supply teacher must make his/her own decision.

It is thus necessary to choose carefully what one wishes to do. The main factors to be considered are:

- How badly do I need this work?
- How confident am I of getting something else if I don't take this job?
- How difficult will the travelling arrangements be?
- Am I happy to work in this school?
- Am I in a position to agree to stay for the period of the assignment?
- How many other jobs have I turned down lately?

These factors will influence the decision the supply teacher makes. The problems the assignment appears to have, e.g. travelling, rough school, out of subject specialism, will be weighed against positive factors, e.g. I need a full-time assignment, I really like this school, there's not much other work around. Whether positive or negative factors carry more weight depends at least in part upon what the supply teacher wants: someone on a pension looking to do a couple of days' work will generally be more put off by negative factors than someone who needs a job to pay the mortgage.

Ultimately, it's your own decision. Especially in the case of awkward assignments, it's worth taking the time to consider seriously whether to take the assignment or to wait for something more suitable.

Mistreatment and recourse

In any case where a teacher feels that he or she has been grossly mistreated by a school, the teaching unions are the obvious recourse. Since contact with the union is generally made through a representative, who is almost always a teacher in one particular school, the supply teacher may not have access to any one particular representative. This difficulty can be overcome in several ways.

Firstly, a good supply teacher will almost certainly 'make friends' with one or more schools. Perhaps these schools' representatives will be able to assist with problems faced in a different institution.

Strictly speaking, this in unnecessary since every teacher has the right to advice from his or her representative, even when only at the school for a half-day. Union representatives represent a union, not a particular school. This is occasionally forgotten, and the need for representation has a depressing habit of occurring in schools where the union officials are not interested in helping outsiders.

If this situation arises, it is worth remembering that there are regional representatives, and that a letter to the regional office can be very effective. The unions have a separate membership rate for those on a daily rate of pay, i.e. supply teachers, but these staff are still full members. They have the same rights to legal representation and other benefits as their full-time colleagues.

Any teacher who does not belong to a union is taking a grave risk and should seriously rethink his or her ideas. Part-time membership for the year costs around fifty pounds. The part-time teacher can save that much on discounted motor insurance alone. It really isn't worth not being a member, not for a morning's pay.

Extreme situations, when things have gone badly wrong and the school will not listen, are fortunately very rare. But what about minor glitches? What can be done before the situation gets out of hand?

It is in fact possible to insure oneself against problems to a great extent. The currency here is not one's hard-earned shekels but professional respect and goodwill. If a school or a particular colleague is impressed with the way a particular supply teacher performs then they will be sympathetic to problems or queries. If the supply teacher arrives on time, checks pupil conduct in the corridors, keeps his or her classes in order and perhaps even volunteers for minor odd jobs here and there then the day they are late or ill, or have a serious incident, their problems will be viewed sympathetically. This is true of permanent staff too, of course. Those who take liberties cannot expect too much understanding when it all goes sour.

Here we return to the question of status. If a supply teacher is well regarded and thought of as part of the department, they will almost certainly receive fair treatment. I have seen schools set up mock interviews, offer references and recruitment advice, and even give a full day's pay for an emergency school closure that saw me home at 10 a.m. This is the hidden benefit of a good rapport with the school; the payoff for a little hard work.

No school feels any obligation to a locum who offers nothing beyond his or her mere presence. Such a person puts nothing into a school and can expect nothing in return. Obviously there are legal requirements which must be honoured, but even so there may be problems if the school feels no loyalty towards the supply teacher.

It is always possible to complain to the agency which sent the teacher. In the case of the LEA, there is only a little help to be had. The supply pool administrators take no responsibility for the teachers they send, nor can they be expected to. If enough complaints are made, the matter might be investigated, but this seems unlikely. Teachers are assumed to be intelligent, capable individuals who can look after their own interests, and to a great extent this is true.

An agency teacher has an advantage, in that while an individual might withdraw his or her services without any real effect on the school, the agency can withdraw the services of all its teachers if necessary. The deputy head who has grown to rely on the convenience of agency teachers will feel the loss and perhaps attempt to remedy the situation. However, there are competing agencies to whom the school may turn instead. It should never come to this, and it very rarely does.

Teachers are competent professionals, and the school management team are all teachers themselves. They will not have forgotten the problems which may affect the classroom teacher, but they might need a gentle reminder of the sort of support that is needed. The supply teacher can help him or herself out by simply behaving as if he or she is part of the school team: asking about potentially difficult circumstances before they occur, requesting support where it is needed and pointing out causes of dissatisfaction before they become major problems. If done tactfully, this approach can solve or avert many potential crises.

As a rule of thumb, the confused supply teacher should remember that he or she is a trained professional. Whether a 30-year veteran or an NQT, he/she deserves a hearing, and should expect one. There is no excuse for allowing a situation to get out of hand by doing nothing and hoping that matters might improve.

A fellow supply teacher or an agency/LEA administrator may well be able to offer advice based upon experience. If this fails, the teacher should discuss his or her problems with the school's union representatives. Even if there is no representative of the supply teacher's own union, most are willing to be helpful, if for no other reason than covert recruiting! Every union member has the right to confidential representation and advice. I have found every representative of every union I have dealt with to be extremely helpful, no matter how trivial the query or how short my acquaintance with the representative.

Failing all of this, the next step is to contact the regional office of whichever union the teacher belongs to. This should not be done until the avenues listed above are exhausted, but it always remains an option. Many of the problems which reach the legal advice stage could have been averted by good practice (teaching or interaction with management) earlier on, or by assertiveness and timely advice. No one has the right to expect a supply teacher to suffer poor treatment simply because he or she is temporary. Most schools will not even consider treating a teacher this way.

But if they do, remember that you do have rights.

CHAPTER NINE

The Status of the Supply Teacher

Once a temporary teacher has been requested, it is assumed that there are obligations between the teacher and the school. Yet no contracts have changed hands; the agency teacher has a contract with the agency and the LEA supply teacher is registered with County Hall, but how exactly does the temporary teacher fit in with the school?

We have already discussed what the supply teacher can expect from the school. Certain rights, like those under the Health and Safety AT Work Act, are protected by law and are not in any way flexible. But what of the great grey mass of professional obligations, rights and duties? The situation is not always clear even for permanent staff.

Is the temporary teacher to be considered part of the school staff for the duration of his/her stay, or is he or she an outsider, present to perform only certain duties? Or is the real situation somewhere in between?

A supply teacher is a professional, a colleague, and in theory an equal to any other member of staff. However, the question of supply teacher status is a rather nebulous one. Agency teachers have a slight advantage here, in that the school has an agreement with the agency itself, which wields more power than the individual and can both offer advice to teachers and also influence schools to a limited extent. The LEA supply teacher is on his or her own.

Agencies make agreements with their client schools, and offer guidelines as to status. One such guideline is more or less as follows: for the first four weeks the locum is treated as being casual, i.e. the school sets work and the supply teacher merely covers lessons with few other duties. The school treats the supply teacher as a filler of gaps and uses him/her for cover in preference to regular staff. The supply teacher will generally have little or no administrative work but can expect no free time.

After four weeks the supply teacher can be expected to set work, mark it, and play an active role as part of the school. He/she should have the same amount of free time for marking as any other teacher, and should attend parents' evenings, write reports etc.

A simple enough guideline, and sensible, yet I cannot remember any school ever actually following it. The reason is not cynical exploitation, nor has it anything to do with incompetence. It is simply that teaching is a profession requiring flexibility. Schools are complicated places, and as a result no guideline is going to be valid even half the time. If a supply teacher is not flexible enough to cope with the changing demands of different schools then he/she is in the wrong job.

The temporary teacher's status depends upon so many variables that it is fair to say that it changes from minute to minute. The most important factors, though certainly not the only ones, are:

- the school's attitude to temporary staff;
- the school's previous experiences with temporary staff;
- the length of the assignment;
- personal factors, e.g. how well the teacher fits in;
- how good a job the teacher is perceived as doing;
- how the supply teacher wants to be treated.

School attitude

The school's attitude is perhaps the main deciding factor. Many schools see supply cover as a way of pasting over the cracks. Pupils must be supervised by a qualified person, and some sort of task must be set to keep them quiet. The responsibility for setting this task is often passed to the supply teacher. In this environment, the locum is merely a means to an end, that end being to avoid disruption to the rest of the school. Such an institution does not want flair and initiative so much as a quiet life. Discipline in the supply teacher's classroom is more important than learning, and colleagues do not want to be burdened with the supply teacher's problems.

This is the 'go in and close the door' situation previously alluded to. It is possible, though superhumanly difficult, to make a school re-evaluate this attitude. Such an attitude feeds off its own results.

On the other hand, a school which expects a supply teacher to take the work hurriedly set by the head of department and extend it, improvise around it and generally use it as the basis for some real teaching, is according the supply teacher the status of a new and temporary, but full-time and valued teacher – thinking of the supply teacher as an educational asset rather than a mere gap-filler and child-minder. Flexibility is required, especially if the teacher is asked to cover a subject outside his/her own specialism. They say that a good teacher can teach anything, and this is the time to prove it!

Many supply staff cheerfully accept the school's preconception of their status and just get on with it. There is nothing wrong with this, but it can sometimes lead to dissatisfaction later in a long-term assignment. Other staff will subtly or openly try to change their status to suit the way they wish to work.

Both approaches are equally valid.

The school's experiences of temporary staff

To some extent, status is determined by those who have gone before and the impression they left behind. People in general have the habit of according the same status to all persons of a particular group. If a school has seen a series of lacklustre performances recently, then the new supply teacher is likely to be regarded in the same way. The opposite is also true and the new supply teacher may find that he/she has a hard act to follow.

There is little the supply teacher can do about these preconceptions except to be assertive and to show the school what he or she can do.

Length of the assignment

Status changes as an assignment goes on. Take for example the fairly common situation where a teacher agrees to come in for a week or so, since the absentee's sick note expires after this period. Then comes the first extension, then the second. The next sick note is for a month. The absence runs on and on. At what point does the supply teacher cease to be an odd-job person and become a full-time, semi-permanent member of staff?

The four-week limit seems to be as good a time as any. The supply teacher has had time to settle in, to find out what he or she is supposed to be doing, to study the syllabus, etc. This is rather important in the case where the supply teacher has agreed to do a few days' cover outside their own specialism. Any competent teacher can administer, say, business studies or history if a specialist sets the work and the supply teacher is willing to put a little effort in. This kind of cover is identical to the internal covers most staff are already familiar with from their permanent post. There should be no real problems with a short cover lasting only a few days.

As time goes on and the cover becomes semi-permanent, the school and the supply teacher must decide whether to continue or to find a specialist. If the teacher continues, then their status has changed from that of a supply teacher, in for a few days to look after some classes, to a member of a department with all the appropriate responsibilities. It is rather important that the supply teacher's attitude changes at the same time, since a department expects different things from a supply teacher than from 'one of its own'.

Of course, the four-week rule is not always valid. One rather harassed department head had me pressed into service as a full member of the department within half an hour. My very next school (six rewarding, challenging and enjoyable months later) wanted only a filler of gaps. I spent nearly three months in this school on a single day cover basis, never being any more than a baby-sitter. Both schools knew exactly what was wanted and it was up to me to decide whether to comply or to bow out gracefully. In neither case was the time factor important, but in some assignments the change in expectations is pronounced. The supply teacher who fails to notice this is heading for trouble.

Personal factors: how well does the teacher fit in?

The supply teacher who is bright, friendly and pleasant is likely to attract favourable attention. This leads directly to more requests to do this or that, but has the advantage that the locum tends to be referred to by name, included in the 'coffee club', invited to visit the pub or the local shops at lunch-time and generally to be regarded as a real human being. The supply teacher who is considered to be a friend as well as a respected colleague is far more likely to be considered important (worth informing about events, for example) and is more likely to be asked back on another occasion.

On the other hand, the dour, grey figure who slumps in the corner of the staffroom, never speaking to anyone except to complain about a pupil or a cold classroom, tends to be referred to as 'the supply'. This sad figure is irrelevant except where his or her actions directly affect others. Even staff who would never consider being rude to someone they knew by name may not worry too much about offending 'the supply'. No one will be disappointed if a different teacher comes in for the next cover.

Such a supply teacher, withdrawn and uninvolved, has done nothing to become part of the staffroom or of the school environment, and has inflicted upon him/herself the status of a mere convenience. Yet it is open to any locum, through his or her own attitude, to become professionally respected and treated accordingly.

How the supply teacher wants to be treated

To some extent, the supply teacher chooses the status he or she is to have. Many are not even aware that they are doing this, yet it affects their whole working life. The subconscious choice is made at the start of every assignment, and several times during it: am I part of this school or merely an unconcerned visitor?

This decision is influenced by the sort of reception the supply teacher receives and by his or her own personal willingness to fit in and contribute to the school. The supply teacher sends signals about how he or she wishes to be treated by the senior staff, or in many cases about how passive he or she is likely to be when faced with senior management requests.

It is easy for a locum simply to be used: loaded with unpleasant, unfamiliar or extra tasks and sent off to have a miserable day. On the other hand, a supply teacher who is willing to be frank about what he or she can and cannot do may well end up bargaining with the deputy head. This should not be seen as disreputable haggling but as a professional discussion, the outcome of which should be a compromise which suits both parties as far as possible. In the interests of good performance it is wise to take on only what the supply teacher can cope with. However, this can be taken to extremes. There is a fine line between 'assertive' and 'stroppy'. Remember that the school has a particular need to fill a certain gap. If one locum is unwilling to do it then another can and will be found. Any compromise must first and foremost suit the school – they are paying the bill, after all.

Conclusion

While working through an agency, I once returned sheepishly to the staffroom after a two-day absence in the middle of a long-term assignment to find that the school had not brought in a replacement supply teacher but had covered internally. Faced with darkly humorous comments along the lines of 'I've been covering the supply teacher's lessons', I expressed puzzlement that a replacement had not been requested from the agency. School policy was to cover the first two days of an absence internally, but in the case where the cost of having a supply teacher in school was being met by the LEA, there seemed no reason not to bring someone else in.

I was informed that it was a question of status. I was not considered to be a supply teacher, but part of the school, and would be treated like any other member of staff. I was hardly in a position to decline a lunch-time duty when asked a week later!

In another school, a teacher found that he received no free time and was being given a great variety of lessons to cover. In short, every odd job in the place was being dumped on 'the supply'. This situation showed no signs of changing as the weeks went by, so the teacher tacitly withdrew his goodwill. Despite ceasing to volunteer, to admit it when he was given Year 11 classes that no longer needed covering; despite setting no work and marking none, this teacher was well regarded and requested by name several times over ensuing years. He remains on excellent terms with the school and is still often used as an odd-job man.

The school had made it plain by its actions that all that was wanted was professionalism and a willingness to cover any lesson. The teacher chose to accept this situation and to do all that was asked of him – but nothing more. This was entirely reasonable and if the senior staff realised what was going on, nothing was said. Of course, this was mainly to do with the fact that the teacher did exactly what was asked of him, and did it well. The school did not ask for initiative, nor acknowledge it when it was shown. A compromise was tacitly evolved and everyone was satisfied.

It is true that under the above circumstances the supply teacher functioned at less than his best possible capacity, but this was all that was asked of him. Since the supply teacher's status was rigidly dictated, after an initial attempt he gave up trying to change it. There was simply no point in accepting extra workload for nothing. It is beyond the scope of this book to discuss the effects of this situation on pupils.

From the two examples above, it can be seen that ultimately the supply teacher's status is a compromise between school and teacher. The school will have an idea about what is required, and though this can be influenced by the teacher's attitude, this position is not really subject to very much alteration.

If a school wishes the supply teacher to function as a full member of a department, then he/she must be treated as such and in this case all rights and duties apply. If a school wants to use the supply teacher to fill every timetable gap then he/she must either do this or withdraw his or her services. However, in this case it is fair to insist that the school sets work, marks it and reports on it.

Any compromise between these two positions must be agreed, either formally or tacitly, between the school and the supply teacher. This may take the form of open negotiation or slightly underhanded 'passive resistance' on the part of the locum, e.g. subtly evading assignments by not being in the staffroom when the deputy head is looking for someone to give the last-minute cover slips to. However, this approach must be used with care, since it is likely to cause irritation and possibly an untimely termination of the assignment if discovered, but it is valuable in those schools which are not prepared to be reasonable about what they ask of temporary staff.

Whatever the school's attitude, a teacher's assumptions about his/her staus have a habit of becoming truth. Just as the school's attitudes can only be slightly altered by the teacher, the reverse is also true. Status is as much a matter of the teacher's choice as the school's.

It is necessary, then, to be aware that this compromise exists, and changes according to the various factors described. The supply teacher must choose how he or she wishes to be treated and act accordingly. It is surprising how often the teacher's choice of status becomes the reality of the situation, even though it is the school management who are in charge.

CHAPTER TEN

Terms and Conditions

Pensions

A retiree who is in receipt of a pension is not allowed to earn more by combination of pension and supply income than his/her previous normal salary. In other words, a teacher who was salaried at £20,000 p.a., who retired on £12,000 p.a., is entitled to earn through supply enough to bring total earnings up to £20,000 in a financial year. Any earnings after this £8,000 are kept, but pension is withheld to bring the teacher's earnings back down to £20,000. In short, the teacher is working for free after this point. However, income earned through agency supply work is not considered for the purpose of pension abatement. The retiree can earn as much as he/she likes, and receive a full pension too.

The Teachers' Pensions Agency offers advice on all matters relating to pension, and can be contacted on (01325) 392929.

Pay

Supply teachers are not on any school's payroll. In order to receive anything more than thanks for your hard work, it is necessary to be registered with an appropriate body, and to prove to this body that you have completed the work you claim to have done. Payment will then be made in due course.

Exactly when this payment will be made depends upon who the supply teacher is being paid by. Most agencies now pay weekly, one week in arrears. Most commonly this is by direct credit transfer to the supply teacher's bank account. Some agencies pay by cheque, some pay monthly, but what they all seem to have in common is prompt payment at the specified time. This is perhaps a benefit of the agencies existing in a competitive market: good teachers are their stock-in-trade and an agency that fails to pay promptly may have to watch its favourite staff defecting to the opposition. This is not to say that problems do not occur, but queries are generally dealt with quickly and efficiently.

The supply teacher is responsible for any delay in getting a timesheet in to the agency office on time. If payroll is run on a Tuesday, and one's time sheet is not posted until then, the supply teacher is to blame and not the agency. This can cause frustration in the case of postal delays, but where one is paid weekly the delay is relatively short anyway.

To be acceptable, an agency timesheet must be signed by the school's authorised signatory. Who this actually is varies from institution to institution. Some schools authorise a senior clerk to deal with payment of supply staff, others require the deputy head in charge of supply cover to sign. A few heads insist upon dealing with all money matters themselves. Once the signature is obtained, the time sheet must reach the agency office somehow. Some schools post them in, others hand the agency copies to the teacher and leave it to him/her to deal with. If neither school nor teacher has any time sheets available, a note typed on the school's headed notepaper should suffice; so long as the school is willing to recognise the bill as legitimate when it arrives, then this will be a satisfactory form of certification that the teacher has completed the required teaching. Once the agency has received the time sheet, the teacher will be paid by the agency and the school will be billed by the agency. This need not concern the teacher.

Teachers working through an LEA also submit time sheets, and are generally paid monthly. Some LEAs have a lamentable record of late payment, lost time sheets and suchlike to rival any horror stories of local government incompetence. Some have been known to pay up to three months after the work was completed. To quote a supply teacher of the author's acquaintance: 'The good thing about working through — LEA is that you can be sure you'll get paid. It's just a question of when.' He added that the average delay was about ten weeks. This situation may be acceptable to retirees who have a pension to live on, but someone working part-time to support a young family, with no other income, is going to encounter problems. There are, to my knowledge, several very good supply teachers who simply cannot afford to work for certain authorities.

It should be noted that many LEAs are prompt and efficient in their payment of their supply teachers. There does not seem to be any pattern to these very different approaches. It is something that we must simply be aware of and react to accordingly.

Basis of payment

There has been much debate and controversy over agency pay and conditions. Some agencies pay to scale point on a pro-rata basis, some pay a fixed rate per day, and some claim to pay to scale point but in fact operate a fixed upper ceiling.

Pay is generally calculated by dividing the teacher's salary by the number of teaching days in the year, and paying this amount (or half of it) for every full day (or half). Thus a typical supply teacher will receive about 1/200th of his/her annual gross salary per full day worked. The flat fees offered by some agencies are towards the lower end of the scale point range. Generally speaking, those at the top end of the salary scale will be short-changed by a flat fee, as this will be much less than their normal daily rate. Those on a very low scale point are being paid more than they would otherwise receive.

A great deal of criticism has been levelled at those taking this approach. Those who use this method have their reasons, though. Apart from a cynical exploitation of the experienced supply teacher in order to make more profit, there are several good reasons why flat fees are offered.

The argument goes like this: the agency charges schools a flat rate for whoever is sent. The fact that one teacher is a retiree with 35 years' experience may not actually make him/her more suitable than a talented and dedicated beginner on Scale Point 1, and the agency has a policy of sending the most suitable candidate, not the most experienced. Further, the agency makes a good deal more profit on someone they have to pay less to. Thus there is a financial incentive for the agency to send out their cheap teachers as much as possible. This results in less opportunities for the older, more experienced locums. Anyone who has seen a post they are perfectly suited for being given to someone less experienced, but much cheaper, will understand this situation.

If the agency takes the financial incentive out of the picture by paying a flat fee, it has no reason to base its choice on anything but suitability. Everyone is playing on a level field and work will be offered to the most suitable supply teachers on merit alone.

There is another argument which goes with this: 'If you can get more money working through someone else, please do. But this is what we're offering. If you're willing to take it, we'll give you plenty of work if you're any good. The choice is yours.'

The supply teacher is quite free to work through whichever LEAs and agencies he/she feels like. Their methods of payment are simply another factor in making a choice.

Pay scales

Teachers' annual salaries increase each year, and with them the daily rate offered by supply agencies and LEAs. It would be pointless to publish a list of daily rates per scale point, as these will be out of date within months. However, remembering that a supply teacher generally receives 1/200th of his/her gross annual salary per day (subject of course to deductions such as tax and National Insurance), in 1998 a supply teacher could expect to earn about £70 per day for someone on Scale Point 0, straight out of PGCE, with no Honours Degree. With a good Honours Degree (2nd class or better) but no experience, £75 per day. Agency flat fees fall in the £75–£80 range. The upper limit for a very experienced teacher working to scale point is about £110 per day.

In addition, some agencies offer a loyalty bonus, an extra payment made if a teacher has worked more than a certain number of days in a given period.

Agency contracts

There are as many different agency contracts as there are agencies, but the terms of engagement are remarkably similar. Many contracts state that they are not 'contracts of employment', i.e. the teacher is not employed by the agency, but are a 'contract of services'. The difference has important legal implications, the upshot of which is that the agency does not employ the teacher but is contracting to find suitable work for temporary teachers, to whom it owes no obligations besides those set out in the contract. Some contracts go on to say that each assignment brief is a separate contract of employment between school and teacher, with the agency acting as a paid middle-man. The contract itself can appear a little daunting and even draconian, but most are merely an attempt to avoid liability for matters beyond an agency's control. As is the case with all contracts, they are statements of duties owed by both parties, and they exist for the protection of both the teacher and the agency.

A typical agency contract will include most or all of the following clauses:

1. **Definitions.**

Most contracts include a clause outlining what the words used within actually mean. This is where such words as 'the client' and 'the locum teacher' are defined.

2. **The contract.**

This section states whom the contract is between and when it is to begin and end. There is often a clause stating that the locum teacher has no right to redundancy or other payments if the contract is terminated or is not renewed for any reason.

3. **Assignments.**

The agency will declare its intent to locate suitable assignments for the locum teacher, and state the terms under which this is undertaken. These commonly include:

- The agency will solely determine suitability of teacher and assignment.
- The teacher accepts that there will be times when work is not available.
- The teacher accepts that the agency has no duty to provide work and that there are no basic hours.
- The teacher is free to accept or decline any offered assignment.
- Upon accepting an assignment, the teacher agrees to abide by the agency's code of conduct and with local working conditions.
- An assignment may be terminated at any time by the agency or the school, without any liability to the locum teacher.
- The teacher is expected to complete the term of the assignment as originally agreed, subject to changes made by school or agency.
- The teacher will inform both agency and school if he/she is unable to work due to illness or some other cause, before a time set out in the contract, e.g. 8 a.m.

4. **Financial matters.**

This section spells out such matters as pay, income tax and any other money-related considerations. Terms usually include:

- when and where time sheets are to be submitted;
- how much the locum is to be paid per day or per half-day. This can be scale-point based or a fixed fee;
- no entitlement to sick pay or holiday pay;
- when payments are to be made, e.g. weekly in arrears;
- that payment will not be made unless a correctly filled time sheet has been received;
- what deductions are to be made, e.g. income tax and DSS NI contributions;
- that there is no pension scheme associated with agency work, and that the teacher cannot claim contributions to the Teachers' Superannuation Scheme.

5. General terms of engagement.

Any general conditions the teacher must agree to. These may include:

- the right of the teacher to be removed from the agency list at any time;
- the teacher's agreement to provide any relevant information such as complaints by the school, health problems or accusations of criminal activity to the agency in a timely manner;
- the teacher's agreement to observe a defined code of practice (see below);
- the teacher's agreement not to accept work directly from a school where the agency has placed him/her, within a set period of being offered work at that school;
- if the teacher is to be covered by any agency-supplied insurance policy;
- the agency is not liable for a teacher's loss of property or injury while on assignment.

Code of practice

Most agencies set out a code which is either included in the contract or referred to in it. The general terms of such a code are as follows:

- The teacher must obey the rules of the establishment he or she is placed in, including instructions from the head teacher or other senior person, in the same way as if he/she were a permanent member of staff.
- The teacher will conform to the school's hours.
- The teacher will comply with all relevant legislation and rules, e.g. Health and Safety and Equal Opportunities policies.
- The teacher will not divulge information about the agency to any third party.
- The teacher will consult with the school ahead of time if possible as to what is to be covered, and where this is not possible be prepared to set their own work in the short term until the situation can be clarified.

- The teacher must be prepared to set and mark work as appropriate, and to undertake all other normal teaching duties such as lunch-time supervision.
- The teacher must not engage in conduct detrimental to the school's interests. This is a blanket clause, and includes such matters as a non-qualified person agreeing to supervise workshop, laboratory or sporting activities for which they do not have the relevant training.

Contracts are complex things, being a way of stating for the legal profession what could be stated to a layman far more simply. The typical contract simply boils down to:

- The agency will try to match the need for temporary teachers with the teachers available. If you don't match any current vacancy, that's not the agency's fault.
- The agency has agreed that the locums it finds for schools will be suitable and will follow a certain set of conduct rules, spelt out in the agency's contract, including the obligation to comply with the school's procedures.
- The agency exists simply to find people to fill vacancies and to handle the administration required by payment etc. It is the school which employs the locum teacher.
- The school's requirements may change. The agency has no control over this and cannot be held responsible.
- The agency agrees to make sure the locum gets paid the amount agreed.
- The teacher is free to do whatever other work is available, but cannot for an agreed period obtain work directly in a school where the agency has arranged a supply posting.

The agency teacher is in a position similar to that of an agented author, or an agency nurse – or an LEA supply teacher. Someone will help find a market for the teacher's skills, but once this is done the teacher is responsible for his/her own conduct. Once contact has been made with a school then the locum is expected to function like any other teacher employed by the school.

In practice, teaching is a profession requiring a great deal of flexibility, and supply teaching is no exception. Quite often a school's requirements may change during the course of an assignment, requiring some direct negotiation between the locum and the person in charge of supply cover at the school. Some schools like to take the home telephone number of a particular teacher and make contact directly. This is not a breach of the agency contract, providing the agency is kept informed of the situation and the teacher still submits time sheets to the agency office. The locum is still working through the agency in this case.

Because any school situation requiring external cover is liable to include a certain amount of chaos, it is not always possible to adhere to the letter of the contract. In fact, the situation is almost never ideal. So long as the concerned parties operate in good faith and try to keep one another informed of what is happening there should be few problems. What agency will protest when you inform them that you've just made some more money for them?

Here is a good example of this sort of arrangement. Early in the term, a particular school requested a supply teacher from the agency to cover a mathematics vacancy. Finding a mathematician was a problem at that time, so the agency telephoned a science teacher who had a reputation for flexibility. The assignment was extended twice and eventually ran for a few weeks. The school was quite satisfied and requested the teacher's home telephone number with the intention of making contact more quickly.

The next time a teacher was required, it was 8 a.m. on a Monday. Urgent cover was needed for a half-day, and possibly more half-days later in the week. The locum was telephoned directly at home, and arrived at the school as quickly as possible, with the result that the agency found out about the assignment when she arrived home at lunch-time. The school had meanwhile negotiated with the locum a three-half-day weekly timetable, covering a mix of mathematics and science, and including the agreement that the teacher would be top of the list for internal covers and might also be asked to stay a whole day or come in on the days when she was not already at the school if the need arose. In short, the teacher was asked to be an odd-job person for the school with a certain minimum teaching commitment. The teacher agreed, subject to not being already committed elsewhere when the call came, then told the agency about the situation.

This may be technically a breach of the letter of the contract, and certainly is more of a problem for the agency to keep track of than the formal request-and-placement procedure. But to the best of my knowledge the arrangement is still ongoing. The school's requirement is being filled by a suitable locum, the agency is still getting its fee, and nobody seems to be complaining.

CHAPTER ELEVEN
Private Tutoring

Many parents feel the need to employ a tutor in the hope of improving their child's examination prospects. While it is fair to say that all that is required for tutoring work is subject knowledge, there is little or no regulation of tutors, which means that anyone can offer to tutor or place a card in the post office window advertising their services. There is no guarantee that the person appointed will be fit to be left alone with children, let alone be able to teach usefully. Without effective regulation the character and ability of some of the tutors available must be considered questionable.

Fortunately, things are not so bad as might be inferred from the last paragraph. Most people offering their services as tutors are qualified teachers or teaching students trying to supplement their income. Others are experts with no teaching qualifications but who possess ability and knowledge in their subject. Sadly, some, including, for example, out-of-work graduates, or musicians who may be good performers, have no idea how to teach, and therefore offer little or no benefit to tutees. However, not all unqualified tutors are poor; some are very good indeed.

Those who are members of the teaching profession will be able to give proof that they hold qualified teacher status, or membership of a teaching union, which should reassure those parents who think to ask about a tutor's credentials. Most are more interested in subject knowledge anyway.

Having decided to offer oneself as a tutor, the first question is how to go about finding tutees. The three most common methods are word of mouth, local advertisement and registering with an agency.

Word of mouth is not especially reliable, but many of us have friends, neighbours or colleagues whose school-age children require some help. Conversely, the question is often asked in staffrooms: 'Do you happen to know anyone who'd be willing to do some maths tutoring?' These personal introductions have the added benefit that the tutor is vouched for by someone known to the tutee or the tutee's parents or carers.

It is quite possible to find tutees by placing a small card in the local post office or newsagent's window, or in a local library. While this method reaches a relatively small client base, most tutees will be local.

Finally, there are now many tutoring agencies, which register a large number of tutors and attempt to match the needs of the tutee with the available resources. There is of course a fee for this service, which is passed along to the client on top of the tutor's fee. Most tutoring agencies cover a fairly wide geographical area, and have nothing to do with supply teaching agencies. Thus far, the two fields have remained separate. Generally, the tutors registered with these agencies are not regulated in any way except that a guideline fee is suggested. Tutors are free to make their own arrangements so long as the introduction fee is paid.

There is no single way in which tutors are expected to operate. Some tutors are willing to travel to their clients' homes while others expect the client to come to them. The fee charged can vary considerably. The going rate is around £12 per hour for GCSE tutoring, £10 per hour for a lower level, say Key Stage 3. For A level or BTEC a rate of around £15 per hour is standard. However, there is no reason why the tutor should not charge more or less than this amount, perhaps to take travel into consideration.

Having found the tutees and agreed what to charge them, the next question has to be: how does one approach tutoring? There is of course no single answer, and the first session often sees the tutor assessing the situation and deciding upon an approach. In many cases the tutee simply 'needs help with his chemistry', so the tutor must use his/her judgement to find strengths and weaknesses, then decide how to enhance or overcome them. Most tutors work one-to-one, and it is desirable to tailor one's style to the needs of the individual.

Most of the demand for tutors occurs on the run-up to GCSE or other examinations. The tutee will probably have revision texts or exercises available. Working through these is as good a method of tutoring as any. In the case of mathematical or technical subjects, one can begin by working through an example, say the first question of the exercise, then guiding the tutee through the next, gradually supplying less and less input unless there are obvious problems. The tutor can then check the answers and show where the tutee went wrong. This method has the advantage that the tutee's homework assignments can be the basis for each lesson. There is nothing wrong with this; homework is set for extra practice and to enable the pupil to become more familiar with the processes and concepts of the course. If the tutor guides the pupil through the work, it is likely that more will be gained from it, so long as the tutor does not let the pupil take a back seat. This is not a matter of doing someone's homework for them, but of assisting the learning process.

Of course, if the tutor prefers, he or she could provide exercises or bring along a suitable textbook to use and let the student take care of his/her own homework.

In the case of less mathematical subjects, the tutor will probably have to go through some areas of the course, explaining tricky concepts and reinforcing current knowledge. There are many excellent revision books available which make a useful resource for this style of tutoring. It is important that the learning be active. Never simply ask a tutee, 'Do you understand?', and accept the answer. Instead the tutor should check by asking suitable questions. It is worth coming back several times to the key elements of the topic. If dealing with, say, respiration, ask the tutee to explain the process without any notes. Fill in the blanks in the explanation, then move on. Ten minutes later, ask again. And again at the end of the session when you spend five minutes summing up.

Leave the tutee with something to do for next time. Something like 'study the topic on photosynthesis again. I'd like you to be able to explain it to me in detail next time.'

It is possible to feel that one is not always giving value for money. Sitting with a revision booklet asking the tutee questions – with the answers in front of you – is something that the tutee's parents or friends can do. So why are they paying you to do it?

The answer is threefold. Firstly, there is the image of professional credibility an outsider arrives with. Many tutees respond better to requests to work or revise a particular topic coming from a teacher than to the same request coming from a parent. Secondly, there is familiarity with various aspects of education. Occasionally the tutee will ask that you help with something completely different, e.g. interpreting a question on history coursework, or suggesting what sort of graph would better represent the geography survey. General teaching experience must be your guide here. There will be some things that you simply cannot help with, but generally the tutor can help out with many aspects of the tutee's education.

Thirdly, and most importantly, it may well be possible for anyone to do what you're doing at the moment, but every now and then the tutee will need a detailed explanation which requires an expert. You should also be able to spot when the tutee does not really know what he/she is talking about and is waffling.

And when he/she suddenly looks up and says, 'Why's that, then?', you can start earning your pay.

To sum up: anyone with subject knowledge can tutor. Doing it effectively requires a certain amount of experience, professionalism and credibility. The latter two you can provide. The former can be learned on the job. There is no need to worry about doing it the right way. All that matters is making sure that the tutee learns whatever is needed.

The right way, then, is whichever way gets the desired results.

CHAPTER TWELVE
Miscellaneous Matters

Pupil management procedures

Most schools have a code of conduct for pupils, and will provide a copy to every supply teacher when he or she arrives. A potted version is often displayed at the front of every classroom, where pupils can see it and be reminded of their obligations. This potted version generally takes the form of a notice bearing a few simple statements such as 'I will treat others with respect' or 'I will do my best to allow all teachers to teach and all pupils to learn'.

The code of conduct will be included within the school's pupil management policy, which is usually available in document form to all staff.

Pupil management policy

The following, based on policies used in several schools, represents a typical pupil management policy.

The policy is aimed at both pupils and staff, and is intended to promote a positive attitude towards discipline in all members of the school community. All members of the school community are encouraged to act with consideration at all times, taking responsibility for their own actions. Pupils are to be made aware that the responsibility for their learning is theirs and does not rest with the teaching staff. Blanket punishments given to a whole group where only a few individuals may be involved are directly contrary to this policy, and should not be used.

The prominent display of a pupil code of conduct is intended to remind pupils of what is expected of them, as is the positive example of staff and prefects. All rewards and punishments given must be employed in a structured manner in keeping with an image of justice and fairness. It is not acceptable to offer rewards for normal good conduct, nor to punish pupils differently for the same offence.

All members of the school community are encouraged to act with proper regard to their own welfare and that of fellow pupils and staff. Staff are encouraged to deal with problems themselves as far as possible. Many potential problems can be avoided by good classroom management techniques. If the situation cannot be resolved then the head of department should be consulted. Pastoral heads (head of house, head of year) should be informed if the problem relates to pupil behaviour or if the situation cannot be resolved. Most behavioural problems require that a referral sheet be submitted to the appropriate pastoral head whenever convenient. If a pupil must be sent to another member of staff then a written note should be sent outlining the situation, and a full referral should follow as soon as possible. A detailed referral should be completed in all cases where it has been necessary to involve other colleagues in any incident.

The senior staff should be informed if the problem is serious or if no other support is available. In an emergency the school office should be contacted for immediate assistance.

Positive reinforcement should be used to reward good conduct and effort in preference to punishment for poor behaviour. Positive reinforcement takes the form of praise, encouragement or rewards such as a good referral. Consistency of approach is vital, as is a balance between encouragement and sanctions. The pupils need to be quite clear that the rules are applied by all staff throughout the school and not just by some of the staff, some of the time.

Marking is a useful tool in maintaining discipline as well as monitoring progress. Good effort and progress should be praised while poor achievement can be dealt with appropriately. Regular careful marking of pupils' books shows that the teacher cares about what sort of effort the pupils make.

The school's hierarchy of sanctions is as follows:

1. verbal warning or reprimand;
2. lines, extra work or other written imposition;
3. detention;
4. withdrawal from classes or loss of privilege – e.g. prefect status withdrawn;
5. pupil placed on report
6. fixed-term exclusion;
7. permanent exclusion.

When reprimanding a pupil, it is necessary to ensure that one does not cause further problems. In many cases a gentle reminder is all that is needed, and anything more will provoke ill-feeling or defiance which will only make matters worse. Any reprimand delivered should avoid insult or sarcasm for similar reasons, and it is vital not to make threats that one either cannot or will not carry out. One should strive to appear calm and reasonable, and should not be drawn into an argument.

If a written imposition is decided upon, this should be suitable to the ability level of the pupil. Lines are quite acceptable, although an essay on an appropriate subject might encourage a more able pupil to think about his or her actions. No more than a page or two should be demanded. Doubling the amount for repeated offences or failure to hand in lines is acceptable, but should not be taken to extremes. Pupils should be observed to ensure that they do not attempt to complete impositions instead of class work.

If a detention is required, pupils may be detained for ten minutes without notice. For a longer detention, parents must be given 24 hours notice. A school detention slip should be obtained, and should be returned countersigned by the pupil's parents. This slip will be filed by the pastoral head.

For more serious or repeated offences, a pupil may be

withdrawn from classes. A detailed referral to the pastoral head is necessary, stating the misbehaviour and whatever actions have already been taken. Department heads may choose to withdraw a pupil from specific lessons if the pupil is considered to be a danger to him/herself or to others, e.g. in technology rooms, or as a sanction at the head of department's discretion.

A pupil may also be placed in school withdrawal, or isolation. This may be for as long or short a duration as appropriate, and follows serious breaches of the discipline code. In this case the pupil will be under the supervision of the duty teacher and work should be provided. Withdrawn pupils will not be allowed to collect their own work, and should have no contact with other pupils. They are permitted to use certain toilets under supervision, but not during lesson changes or break times.

A pupil may be placed on report to monitor attendance, attainment, punctuality, behaviour or at parental request. Pupils on report should sit at the front of the class and must present the teacher with their report at the beginning of the lesson. Reports should be completed at the end of the lesson and will be filed by the pupil's pastoral head.

Where a pupil is excluded, this may be for a fixed term (no more than 15 days per term) or permanently. Exclusions must be sanctioned by the head teacher. Fixed term exclusions are usually reserved for major infractions such as bullying, theft, vandalism, verbal abuse to staff, and other behaviour where a cooling off period is necessary. Permanent exclusion is reserved for situations where all other sanctions have failed or a very serious offence has been committed.

The course of the day

On arrival

- Be on time or a little early.
- Have a few backup lesson plans, pens and paper with you.
- Be prepared for a sudden change of plan.

- Find out who you need to see about work and resources.
- Find out about the school's discipline system.

During each lesson

- Insist that the pupils follow normal school procedures, e.g. coats off in classrooms.
- Don't just sit at the front. Move around the room and help/chivvy pupils along.
- Don't let pupils wander around, shout out, or rake in cupboards.
- Don't get drawn into conversation or argument.
- Deal with problems swiftly and don't let them escalate.
- Clear up in good time and get back everything you loaned out.
- Step out into the corridor at lesson change and make sure pupils move about in an orderly fashion.

At the end of the day

- Write up concise notes for the regular teacher.
- Leave the room tidy.
- Spare a few minutes for a debrief with the head of department or other colleagues.

Assessing your performance

As remarked earlier, much of supply teaching is a matter of starting from scratch every day. For this reason there is a very strict limit to what can be targeted and what can be observably achieved. One cannot truly expect to win the hearts and minds of the pupils on a one-day cover.

Thus, when leaving an assignment, it is worth considering what realistically could have been achieved and attempting to compare your achievements with that, instead of against some ideal of perfect teaching.

There are questions you can ask yourself. Try to look at your day from the point of view of an outsider – say a pupil sitting in the middle of the classroom – and answer them honestly:

- Did I remember what I was told at the beginning of the day about work, discipline, school policies, etc?
- Did I apply what I was told?
- Did I attempt to teach rather than baby-sit?
- Did I make my instructions clear and concise?
- Did I attempt to appear firm, but good-humoured and reasonable?
- Did I uphold good practice as regards discipline and classroom conduct?
- Did I do my best to help the pupils learn from today's lesson?

The more you can answer 'Yes', the better your performance has been. Conversely, it is to be hoped that you can answer 'No' to the following:

- Was I arbitrary and bad-tempered with pupils?
- Did I come over as uninterested in the pupils' work and welfare?
- Have I left a mess (physical or situational) for colleagues to clear up?

Overall, it is necessary to be realistic about your performance. You will have bad days. There will be times when you stagger out of a classroom wondering if any teaching ability you may once have had has completely deserted you. If you understand the reasons why the disaster happened you will be able to learn from the situation. It may simply have been because many pupils see supply teachers as fair game, an opportunity to mess about. You may have asked for trouble by taking the wrong approach with certain classes, by coming over as confused and disorganised, or by not asking for help when it was obvious you needed it. Bearing in mind that pupils are generally more inclined to give a teacher they don't know a hard time, especially when that teacher may not be around long enough for there to be any comeback, if you managed to keep reasonable order in the classroom, to get at least some of the pupils through the set work, and did not allow matters to get out of hand, then you may have done as well as could be expected. Strive for more, but be aware of the best that can realistically be achieved and compare your performance to that.

Occasionally, though, you'll have a great day, when everything works perfectly and the light-bulbs are visibly coming on above the pupils' heads as you rattle through the syllabus in fine style. Days like this do happen, when all expectations are exceeded. When it happens, don't be smug. Instead, ask yourself, 'Why?'

CHAPTER THIRTEEN

Forms and Documents

This chapter contains several document blanks which can be photocopied for use as desired. The purpose of these forms is to assist the supply teacher in approaching each assignment in as organised a fashion as possible. Permission is granted to copy any of the forms within this chapter for personal use only.

The Booking Form is intended as an aid in keeping track of where to be, when, and how to get there. Essential details of the institution, as well as a reminder who booked the assignment in order to send the time sheet to the right place, can be filled in and filed, along with those all-important directions and A-Z reference. Any notes such as a request for a preliminary visit or the possibility of changes to the assignment can be recorded.

The Record of Assignments is intended to be filed in the supply teacher's records. It serves as a reminder of when and where the supply teacher has worked and any special circumstances which arose, and can be used to help keep track of which payments may be outstanding.

A file filled with such forms will prove very useful as proof of experience when discussing scale points with a new institution, agency or LEA. Details can be quickly checked if necessary, ensuring the supply teacher can claim an appropriate salary.

The third form, Lesson Notes, is a watered-down lesson plan, with room to make a quick note of which class is to be taught and where, what time the lesson starts and finishes, what the set work is about and where to find it. A section for notes at the end can be used to record how far the class got with the work, problems or commendations, etc.

The fourth form, End-of-Cover Notes, is intended to provide the school with a concise description of what the supply teacher has done in a period of cover, whether this was a morning or a term. A simple note on which topics were covered, perhaps referring to syllabus documents, and a general note on class behaviour, will be a big help to the returning teacher.

Schools have their own incident and accident forms, usually obtainable from the office or head of department. These should be filled out as soon as possible after any accident or serious incident. However, in case the situation does not require a legal document, or one is not readily available, the Incident Report form can be used. Any incident which the teacher deems is serious, and certainly any accident or situation requiring the intervention of another member of staff, should be documented in case of future problems. The form provided is general enough to cover most eventualities.

Booking Form – School Details

Name of school _____

Address _____

_____

_____

_____

Contact name _____

Telephone _____

Report to _____

At (time) _____

Booked by _____

Date to commence _____

Duration of assignment _____

Subjects to be covered _____

_____

_____

A–Z reference _____

Directions _____

_____

_____

_____

_____

_____

_____

Notes _____

_____

_____

_____

_____

_____

_____

Record of Assignments

School/Institution _____

Address _____

_____

_____

Telephone _____

Dates of assignment _____

Working through/to be paid by _____

Subjects and year groups taught _____

_____

_____

_____

Notes _____

_____

_____

_____

Payment received? _____

School/Institution _____

Address _____

_____

Telephone _____

Dates of assignment _____

Working through/to be paid by _____

Subjects and year groups taught _____

_____

_____

Notes _____

_____

_____

_____

Payment received? _____

Lesson Notes

Date and duration of cover _____

Period _____ Times _____
Class _____ Room _____

Lesson content _____
_____
_____
_____
_____
_____

Notes _____
_____
_____
_____
_____
_____

Period _____ Times _____
Class _____ Room _____

Lesson content _____
_____
_____
_____
_____
_____

Notes _____
_____
_____
_____
_____

End-of-Cover Notes

Teacher _____ Dates of Cover _____

Class _____

Topics covered _____

_____

_____

Notes _____

_____

_____

_____

Class _____

Topics covered _____

_____

_____

Notes _____

_____

_____

_____

Class _____

Topics covered _____

_____

_____

Notes _____

_____

_____

_____

_____

Incident Report

Name of teacher _____

Date, time and place of incident _____

_____

Other persons involved _____

Details of incident _____

_____

_____

_____

_____

_____

_____

Action taken _____

_____

_____

_____

_____

_____

_____

Matter referred to _____

_____

_____

Resolution/feedback _____

_____

_____

_____

_____

_____

_____

Index